Second Coming

Awakening The Christ Within

Kimberly Lilith Phelps

Second Coming
Awakening the Christ Within

© 2017 Kimberly Lilith Phelps
ISBN 978-0-9883597-5-8
Library of Congress Number 2016943339

A Soul Proprietorship, LLC
PO Box 27182
Golden Valley, MN 55427
WherePathsCross@gmail.com
www.WherePathsCross.net

All rights reserved. Printed in the US. No part of this book shall be used or reprinted in any manner without written permission.

This book could not have happened without
the Bible Boys and the Psychic Sorority.
Thanks, y'all.

Acknowledgements

You would not be holding this book in your hands were it not for these people:

Mark Beidelman and Tammera Logan who held the space when this book was only a Vision.

My editor Tim Miejan, who understood how hard it was for me to let this baby go and who held it in reverent, capable, and loving hands.

Those who read my early manuscripts, especially Jane Heller, Jason Berger, Tammera Logan, Natalie Dousette-Aiello, Teresa McMillian, and Dawn Turner. Special thanks to Theresa Phelps, who went above and beyond the call.

Tammera, Natalie, and Teresa for being "my own personal TNT." You held me together when the fear was more than I could handle.

All the people who contributed to the Spiritual conversations at "Beer and Bibles at Bunny's," especially Ted Schwarz, Barry Marks, Nancy Schwarz, Pete Simpson, Chris Winter, Jason Berger, Katherine Poindexter, Dan Akins, and Amy Cotter.

Thank you, Barbara With, for layout, cover design, publishing support, unending friendship against all odds, and for showing me that I Am simple and beautiful.

Thank you, Teresa, for loving me for over 30 years as I struggled to find the bridge and stand strong once I found it. And Ted, for joining me on the bridge and teaching me about both sides. People told me I couldn't write a book to two different audiences. The two of you helped me figure out that it's not two audiences ... It's one audience speaking in two different languages.

"And the last shall be first." To my incredible family, thank you for ... everything! The most important thing I learned during this process is that nothing is more valuable in this life than Love, especially the undying Love of family. It may look messy sometimes but at least we do it with passion! Clay and Mason, Katie and Dan, Scott and Sam – There would be no me without you. "These are days we'll remember."

Table of Contents

Introduction i
   Search For Meaning ii
   Friends On A Bridge iv
   Oh, My God v
   Structural Details vii

Preface: How I Got Jesus Back 1
   Yes, Jesus Loves Me 2
   Spiritual, But Not Religious 4

Taking the Bible Literally 7
   ... But Then Why Did Jesus Speak in Parables? 7
   Divine and Human 8
   We're Not Worthy? 10
   Developing a Spiritual Practice 12
   The Paradox 14

Setting a Foundation 17
   Before the Beginning 17

When Would NOW Be a Good Time? 19

God is Still Talking 23
   Hearing God's Voice 24
   What's It Really Like? 27

The Word 29
   Transactional Theory of Literary Work 30

Inner Dance 31

Agendas 37
   Hidden and Otherwise 37
   The Biggest Lies 38
   The Unconditional Love of God, The Father 40
   "Don't Look Where You Don't Want to Go" 41

My Agenda 43
   What's It Really Like — What Do I Do? 45

Jesus, The Christ and Us 47
   Created In the Image of God 47
   To Pick Up Our Power 51

Journey Toward Wholeness 55
   Call Your Father 56
   To Empty Yourself 60

The Most Important Thing 63

Why Did the Messiah Come? 69
   It Is Finished 70
   He Takes Away the Sin of the World 71
   What's It Really Like to Love Our Enemies? 73

Shifting Our Perceptions 75
   Sin and the Mind-Body Connection 77
   We All Fall Short 78
   Believing We Are Separate
      is a Temptation of the Flesh 79

The Dark Side 81
   Picking Up Our Power 82
   "The Way" 84

I AM The Way, The Truth and The Life 87
   Detachment is the Ability to Not Be Offended 90

God is 95
   God Gathers All the Children 95
   Jesus Was Radical 97
   Radical Love Can Save Us 100
   When I'm afraid 100
   To Love the Way God Loves 102

Ego, Fear and Getting Un-stuck 105
   Striving For Balance 110
   The Ability to Change 111
   Healing Inner Conflict 112

Our Human Ego 113
   Sneaky Ego 115
   When Fear Is In the Driver's Seat 117

Ego and Depression **119**
   Deep, Dark Work 121
   Developing a Spiritual Practice: What Do I Do?... 123
   Light in the Darkness 124

Out There and In Here **127**
   Developing a Spiritual Practice: What Do I Do?... 129
   "Inside" 130
   About This Poem, and Writing
      or Journaling In General 132
   What's It Really Like? Real-life Doubts and Fears 133
   A Note About Speaking the Truth 135

Keeping Tabs on the Ego **137**
   Faith When We're Afraid 141
   Memo From God: "The Gift is Never Given
      in Only One Direction" 143
   Developing a Spiritual Practice: What Do I Do?... 144

Heaven on Earth **147**
   To Walk on Water 147
   Manifestation and the Law of Attraction 150
   Forgiving Others—Judgment and Forgiveness 151
   "Judge Not Lest Ye Be Judged" 153
   Forgiving Ourselves First 154
   The Greatest Lies Are the Ones We Tell Ourselves 156

What's the point, really?
   Kobayashi Maru 157
   "Reality is Free. It's the Illusion You
      Have to Pay For" 159

Picking Up Our Power **161**
   God's Will and Our Call 164
   What's It really Like Healing Inner Conflict?
      To Really Pick Up Your Power? 165

Letting Go of the Title "Sinner" **167**
   Memo From God 168
   Grace or Works — How About Both! 169

Beginning of the End **171**
   Learning By Example 174

Genesis Revisited **177**
   There's Only One of Us Here 178
   Made of God 180
   God, the Creator and God, the Created 182

A Creation Story **183**
   Adam and Eve 183
   Inherently Good 184
   Inherently Evil? 187
   The New Covenant 187
   Namaste 190
   Developing a Spiritual Practice: What Do I Do?... 192

The Next Beginning **193**
   What If Jesus Really is the Man at
      the Gas Station? 193
   The Bridge 195
   The Last Shall Be First 196

Remember ye not the former things,
neither consider the things of old.
Behold, I will do a new thing;
Now it shall spring forth.
Shall you not know it?
Do you not perceive it?

Isaiah 43:18-19

Introduction

I see myself standing on a bridge. On one side are the Spiritual People and on the other side are the Christians. Can there be peace in the middle, I wonder? Well, I'm in the middle and I have found peace, so it must be possible. At first I have my hands extended out to either side, since I embrace both of these traditions in my personal relationship with God. Then God says to me, "Lily, bring your hands together at your heart in Namaste, as in prayer." Namaste is a respectful greeting: with the hands in prayer gesture, we bow to the other and inwardly express, "The God in me honors the God in you." No details, no discussion, no test to pass first. By simply honoring the Light of God as it shines from each of us to the other, we begin to see every person as a piece of the same Spirit that illuminates all of our lives. This is key if we are ever to live in peace with one another. This is how Jesus lived and this is what The Christ has brought into my life. This is what God calls me to share with you now.

Second Coming

I have spent more than 30 years of my life being "Spiritual but not religious." In these pages you will hear about my journey as I changed from being a child who loved Jesus into an adult with misunderstanding and anger — not with God but with the Church. My experiences with others who claimed I was doing God wrong became a stumbling block for me. This is the story of my rebirth. I have come full circle, back to an entirely new relationship with God.

After having left the Church, I found my way on the other side of the bridge. Here people called God things like Divinity and Creator, Higher Power, the Universe and Spirit. Here nobody tried to tell me what my God had to look like or how I had to act in my relationship with the Divine. What I have learned is that God by any other name is still God. And I have learned that it is time for us to put away our childish squabbling over details and differences and rise up in the love that our Creator intends for us. It's a choice and an invitation: to love or not to love. Simple, direct, and sometimes nearly impossible to do.

Search for Meaning

Our lives are not always easy and sometimes our lives are truly horrible, so we search for meaning. A way to find meaning in my existence came when I started to realize that the tough stuff is meant to teach us and to make us stronger. We are not being punished. We are being educated through our experiences and often we learn best from those that are the most difficult and painful. This doesn't make us bad. This makes us instruments of God

Introduction

— important elements in the Divine Plan! When Jesus said that the most important thing is that we learn to love, he knew this was the only thing that would save us and bring us together — with one another and within ourselves. He knew love was, and is, the Truth. Only by love and for love can we advance in the ways God intends.

This message came to me through Jesus — perhaps not the Jesus of my childhood but Christ just the same. In all the years I spent away from the Christian Church, standing with clenched fists much of the time, I never imagined that a Christian church and the people who worship there would help bring my story full circle. The people of the Episcopal Church have changed the face of Christianity for me and in doing so, they helped heal the anger I held toward Christians for most of my life. Now, mind you, I wasn't angry with God and I always loved Jesus. It was Christians I had a problem with.

In this book I illustrate how Jesus has guided me as I stumbled around and tried to figure out how to be happy in a troubled world, how to live a life aligned to the highest good, how to get my needs met, and how to leave things better than I found them. I have had to learn how to take responsibility for my own choices and how to make honorable decisions in a culture that often teaches us to find someone else to blame for what we don't like. I'm learning how to love myself exactly as God made me, in the face of all my human doubts, fears, and flaws. My hope is that my story will help you do the same.

I also hope this writing will bring my friends on one side of the bridge closer to peace with my friends on the other side of the bridge — not by giving up anything they believe and hold dear but by realizing that The Christ stands at the center of us and that Jesus taught us how to find peace in God.

Friends on the Bridge

When I talk to my friends on each side of this bridge, I actually make reference to two groups of people:

- The Spiritual People, many of whom pushed the Church away just as I did, may not realize that many of the spiritual principles we practice are present in the Bible and the teachings of Jesus. In this book I illustrate some of the teachings of Jesus that are messages about what Spiritual People call the Christ Consciousness.

- The Christians, many of whom think the Spiritual People just don't get it or just don't care, might be surprised to find that there are other ways — deeply profound and reverent and beautiful ways — to celebrate God in the world. Just because some of us have been hurt by the more fundamentalist aspects and actions of religion doesn't mean we don't love God and don't connect with Jesus deeply.

When we are reading and discussing in my weekly Bible study, I often say, "Ya know, the Spiritual People believe that, too, but they call it by another name …" And when I'm with my Spiritual friends I say, "Ya know, that's in the Bible. Jesus said it this way …" My friends on both sides of the bridge

Introduction

will tell you that I'm also very fond of saying, "Ya know, there's a Country Western song about that." You have to watch out for me or I'll have you lovin' Jesus, chatting with God, and humming a song all at the same time!

For me, this works. I have finally arrived at a place in my life where I don't need anyone to agree with me, because I'm full and rich and completely happy in my relationship with God — and that's all that matters in the end. Having healed my anger and found my way back to peace, I can now talk to just about anybody and show them new ways to look at how the Creator moves in our lives. I'm writing about it in the hope that we can begin to build a bridge of peace for the whole world.

Oh, My God!

I know these are big statements and by now you might be wondering what you've gotten yourself into. When I first started working on this book, I was guided to the title, *Second Coming*. Imagine yourself in my shoes: God calls you to write a book that, if anybody reads it, will probably be controversial. God says to talk about a new understanding of the words of the Bible and of Jesus when he spoke of The Christ and the Spirit of Love that exists within all people. No big deal, right? I was terrified. But having heard and followed this voice for many years, I knew this voice was from God and that arguing with my Creator was not a terribly effective use of my time and energy. So I started to write.

To keep myself somewhat sane early in this process, I created another title that calmed me down: How I Got Jesus Back. This helped a lot.

Second Coming

It was smaller. Less intimidating. And it was more personal. Now I was able to write from the perspective of my own story and my relationship with God without thinking too much about the bigger picture of the Second Coming and all the implications of the words I was being compelled to say. I simply thought of this book as being about the second time Jesus came into *my* life — after I left the mainstream Church.

So I'm here to tell my story, with all its human flaws, struggles, doubts, and fears. I share how tough these concepts were for me to grasp at first — trusting that you can find your way as well. As you will hear me say many times, I'm not special. I'm a strong, ordinary woman who has done a *lot* of work to get where I am today. This journey has not been easy for me and I still fall down every single day. Knowing that I have a purpose, that I am part of something bigger than myself, that I have a relationship with my Creator, and I am cared for no matter how badly I mess up makes it easier to get back up and move forward in love instead of fear.

Know that it is never my intent to tell you what your relationship with God *should* look like, simply because of how mine looks. I don't know your story. I don't know how your spiritual journey will unfold for you. And because I know the beauty is in the unfolding, I wouldn't tell you if I could. It is through the process of discovery that we all figure out who we are and what we want our lives and our relationships to be. That's what makes life such a grand adventure.

An important reason for including stories from my personal journey in this book is to give you an idea of how to apply mystical spiritual ideas to a real human life. Mystical experiences, by virtue of their inherent Divinity, are beyond our understanding. By telling my story and by sharing what I've experienced when other people have done similar spiritual work, I hope to create a road map for you. Whether you follow the map or not, I hope you find my examples helpful and even motivational. In other words, "Please try this at home!"

Structural Details

- In this book when I speak of experiences at "my church," I am referring to the Episcopal Church, of which I have been a member for several years. I also refer to the spiritual church with which I was involved for more than 15 years. For clarity, I will always refer to this group as "my Spiritual Community" to clearly distinguish it from my Episcopal Church. When I speak generally of "the church," I am speaking of the mainstream Christian Church or mainstream religion — and when I speak of fundamentalist Christians, I have made every attempt to make it very clear that these remarks are not about *all* Christians. At no time do I intend to define any of these groups for you or say that one group is wrong and another is right. It is not my right nor do I have the ability or desire to do that. I merely give a declaration of my experience with each of these groups.

- Another important notation is about Synergy Alliance, an organization I helped create in the 1990s. I refer to Synergy Alliance several times throughout the text. My spiritual life began in 1993 due in no small part to my association with two women: Barbara With and Teresa McMillian. Teresa and I had been best friends for 10 years when we met Barbara. None of us had any idea that we would be together on a journey that would change our lives forever. I am eternally grateful to these two women and I thank God every day for bringing us together and for helping me deepen my relationship with God while walking beside the two of them.

- One final note about my writing style: I often use capitalization as a form of emphasis — and even reverence. Yes, I know this is technically incorrect and I have made every effort to conform to the rules of proper writing technique in this work but sometimes I just can't help myself. For me, words like "Soul" and "Spirit" and "Self Love" are simply too important not to be capitalized. I capitalize the word Spiritual, just as anyone would capitalize the word Christian.

Preface

How I Got Jesus Back

The ideas in this book may seem radical to you. For much of my life they would have seemed radical to me as well. But then God came to me in a startlingly different way and asked me to look with new eyes at some of the oldest of truths. This is the story of my awakening — a story that has taken over fifty years in this lifetime to unfold.

In framing these "new-old" ideas, I use my own personal story. I do this not because I'm special but precisely because I'm not. I'm just like you: an ordinary person who has lived a fairly ordinary life. I've always sought to live my life in accordance with what I believe to be the highest good. I love God and I want to be a good person and it's not always the easiest thing to do. Hopefully by reading about how I've tried to apply these ideas to my own life, you will gain better insight into how you might apply them to yours.

I also use my story because it is the only story I have the right to tell. I don't consider myself an expert on anything. I'm not a Biblical scholar or a soon-to-be Ascended Master. I'm a regular person who believes that the Bible and the teachings of Jesus are relevant to my daily life and are important tools to help me live better. I'm willing and able to tell my own story, after having done a significant amount of study and self-scrutiny and my life has improved greatly as a result of the spiritual healing work I've done. We can all learn from one another by sharing our life stories, so this book is a compilation of some of the most important pieces of my life and an exploration of how I have learned to walk in this world. It presents the idea that strong, ordinary people can change the world. We do it one person at a time, starting with ourselves.

Yes, Jesus Loves Me

I have always loved Jesus. I was that "weird kid" who went to church not because my parents made me go, but because I really *wanted* to go. I was told that God was there in church, so I went to see Him at His house. (I didn't know yet that God could be found in lots of other places.) We sang, "Yes, Jesus loves me," and my mother taught us to live by the Golden Rule: *"Do unto others as you would have them do unto you."*[1] I truly believed both of these ideas.

In my early twenties, I became disillusioned with organized religion and the mainstream Church. Religion seemed to divide people more than unite them. Various dissenting groups seemed so sure that they were the only ones who had it right. I thought about all the people who have died in the name of God. I watched as Christians spoke ill of one another and judged others, rather than

---

[1] Luke 6:31

Preface

looking at the way they were living their own lives. In the end, I got tired of Christians who didn't act much like Christ. To me it seemed to miss the entire point.

I didn't know how to react to what I was feeling and I was tired of people telling me that I had to do what *they* said or I was surely going to burn in hell. People who beat me about the head with a Bible while claiming I was doing God wrong just pushed me further away from the Church — any church. The idea that Jesus would only love me under certain man-made conditions didn't make sense to me. "Yes, Jesus loves me, but only if ...?" That isn't how the song goes. And so I pushed the Church away — and I became increasingly angry with Christianity for taking Jesus away from me.

But I had a little secret. I have always held Jesus in my heart. It was as though I thought that if the Christians found out, they'd take him away from me for good. So I loved him in secret for much of my life.

It wasn't until my late thirties that God started showing up in my life in new and miraculous ways. First I had a Spiritual Awakening, an experience of the Divine that transcends conscious, human understanding. (This experience is similar in feeling, although perhaps not in detail, to what Christians might describe as being "Born Again.") I began to understand that Jesus taught self-responsibility, self-empowerment, and Self Love. Slowly I began to "come out of the closet" about my unconventional relationship with God.

Shortly after my Spiritual Awakening, my two best friends and I were reading from a book called *The Urantia Book,* one of many texts used

Spiritual, But Not Religious

Fifteen years prior to joining the Episcopal Church, I was a very involved member of a Spiritual community and for several years I participated in church leadership. That particular community states its purpose as: "Honoring all paths to the Divine."

Spiritual people who don't follow a specific religion often refer to their personal *spiritual practice*. A *practice* can mean many things: an individual covenant with God or the Divine, a personal path of awakening, a particular way of experiencing the Universe, etc. The difference between a spiritual practice and belonging to a religion is that one person's spiritual practice may not look like anyone else's. Spirituality is about finding what works for you *and* honoring what works for everyone else. Until I joined this Spiritual community, I had never experienced an entire congregation that supported individuals in this way. It was wonderful to feel safe and accepted as I learned a new way to experience my relationship with God.

The group identified as "Spiritual, but not Religious" represents the fastest-growing segment of the religious demographic. In *Christianity After Religion*,* Diana Butler Bass reveals that "… the number of Americans who claim no religious affiliation has doubled since 1990." Bass speaks of the current spiritual awakening as the "New Light," contrasting it with the "Old Light" ("… those who ignore or resist change") of the doctrinal church model. She says, "Historians, journalists and critics have named [this awakening] everything from the 'Next Christendom' to the 'Great Emergence,' claiming that [it] marks the most significant change in the Christian faith since the Protestant Reformation."

**Christianity After Religion*, Diana Butler Bass, 2012

Preface

by spiritual people. This book told us that Jesus came into the world to anchor love in a whole new way. It further stated that after Jesus died, Paul and others created the new religion, Christianity, based on the worship of Jesus. But Jesus never said, "Worship me." Jesus, who said that he came from God and we come from God, also proclaimed, *"Greater things than I have done you will do."*[2] He said that we will be judged as we judge each other[3] and that the most important thing is simply to *"Love God and love your neighbor as yourself."*[4] Suddenly I came to the realization that nobody owns Jesus and nobody owns Truth. In that one amazing instant, I got Jesus back! I didn't have to love him in secret anymore. I knew him and he knew me and we could have our relationship without anyone else's permission. I no longer needed to live by someone else's definitions. From that moment on, I was free!

At this same time I met a fundamentalist Christian who became what I called my "sparring partner." We explored the Bible together, each finding a somewhat different truth from our study of the same words. The differences in our interpretations were subtle but very profound. At first I didn't realize that he was simply repeating to me what he had been taught at his church. But what I did understand fairly quickly was that all of his interpretations — from what he was taught in church to what he heard in his own mind when he read the words in the Bible — came to him through a filter of unworthiness. With the belief that he

---

2	John 14:12
3	Matthew 7:1
4	Mark 12:30-31

would never be good enough for God, he found exactly what he expected to find in the Bible: sin, shame, guilt, doubt, fear, etc. (I'll share more about these preconceived notions and beliefs later in the book. We *all* have them to varying degrees and sometimes just recognizing your own preconceived notions will release you from them, making you more able to access Divine love in what you hear and experience.)

As these realizations dawned on me, so did another: I was actually giving voice to a new understanding of the meaning of these very old words. *How could this be?* I began to wonder. Thus began my study of the Bible using my "new eyes" and my newfound connection to God, who existed not just in a church but also in my heart.

Taking the Bible Literally

... But Then Why Did Jesus Speak in Parables?

There are those who take exception to other possible meanings or interpretations of the words in the Bible. These people say, "We take the Bible literally." My response? If that works for you in your relationship with God then that is a beautiful thing! It simply didn't work for me. Fortunately, God found me another way.

The problem with insisting on a literal interpretation is that we cannot possibly know the literal meaning of everything in the Bible. We can *decide what we think is literal,* but my version of literal and yours might differ greatly. Also, life is so different now compared to when the Bible was written. We certainly do not follow some of the cultural norms of that time anymore. For example, do we think women should never to be permitted to teach men? Does "spare the rod and spoil the child" mean that we are supposed to literally beat our children with sticks? Do we really have to sacrifice animals and do burnt offerings in order to be holy? No, it doesn't always work in the literal sense.

Personally I prefer the depth of meaning afforded by opening to paradox and metaphor, which involves the use of figurative language, allegory, and parable. Jesus spoke in parables — and this is where the richness and the challenge comes into the process of learning to live from his words. *We have to think and we have to make choices!* In my experience the Bible actually has more depth of meaning when we open to other possibilities within the text. The word "allegory" is defined as "a representation that both parallels and illustrates something deeper." An example of allegory given in the dictionary is the story of the search for the Holy Grail, which also illustrates an inner spiritual search. In this example, if stories about the Holy Grail are only taken literally and the meaning is restricted to the search for an ancient cup, nobody will ever find anything. Jesus knew this and he formed his messages so they would speak to people in all walks of life and remain relevant over time.

Throughout this work, let's continue to explore the depth of meaning afforded by looking deeper — beyond the literal.

Divine and Human

I give new witness to old truths. The truth I speak of is as old as God, the Creator, the one who set everything in motion. What is this "new-old" truth? Simply that in this life we are both Divine and human. These two aspects of Being exist in symbiotic relationship to one another for a finite length of time: the length of each human life. At the end of each life, the human body ceases to live and the Divine Spirit continues on as it always has — without the vehicle of the body — into eternity. This physical human life is temporary; Spirit, Soul, or what I refer to as The Christ, is eternal. And what the Soul experiences during the time it inhabits a physical body is necessary to the development of Divine Spirit.

Jesus came to help us get the most out of this symbiotic relationship, teaching that the key to living a full, rich, healthy life is to learn to love. This may sound simple, but unlike him, we are not yet able to be fully conscious of the Divinity we all hold. He wanted to help us have greater awareness and make more use of our own Divinity in the presence of the human ego. In this way we can recognize and experience a new paradigm of life in Christ. Being made of the eternal energy of God — as experienced in the context of a physical human life — we begin to realize that it is difficult if not impossible to fully experience one without the other. This is important. When we put too much focus on one or the other — be it Divine Spirit or the physical human experience — we get out of balance and life becomes more difficult.

Jesus did not come in human form simply to be worshipped. He came to set an example, to be a teacher and to show us a better way to live. He was a living, breathing human being who was completely aware of his Divine Spirit. He came to demonstrate how to balance Divinity and humanity. The assignment he left for us was that we learn to do the same. With this understanding, we can start to see that when Jesus said, "follow me," he did not mean "worship me." He meant, "You are just like me. Be like me."[5] Jesus was telling us to take

---

5   1 John 3:2-3 and Philippians 2:5-8

full and complete responsibility for who and what we are, just like he did. He was saying, "Watch; I'll go first and then you follow me. And when you're frightened or you don't know what to do, I will hold your hand because *"I Am with you always."*[6]

This truth seems new, only because many of us have not been taught to keep it alive in our hearts. Instead we have been told the Big Lie: that we are not good enough, and that even God finds us undeserving. This lie was passed on to us by those who believed it themselves and proclaimed it to everyone else. And we accepted it. We bought this Big Lie, and we are living it out in more ways than we can imagine. Now it is time to let it go.

We're Not Worthy?

Feeling unworthy is universal to the human experience. This is what healing and learning Self Love is all about for me: learning to believe, deep down, that I am worthy of being loved by God, by myself, and by those around me.

God made us. How dare we think ourselves unworthy of love? Wouldn't it be better to strive to love as God has taught us? And perhaps doing this will actually help us learn to feel worthy.

Let our first act be to pray for those who do not believe themselves worthy of love — from God, themselves, or anyone else. This includes all of us some of the time, some of us most of the time, "and a few of us all of the time," as one of my friends noted.

---

[6] Matthew 28:20

Taking the Bible Literally

May each of us in our own time and in our own way, learn to connect with Divine love and with our own Divinity. When you put infinite Divine Spirit into these fragile, frightened human bodies, things can get messy. But we have a choice about how we experience this life. It is time to acknowledge who and what we truly are. We need to stop waiting for something or someone to come along someday and "save us." We need to start living in and from the essence of The Christ, right here and right now. We need to know that we are part of God's dream and that we are called, in the flesh, to make God's word manifest in this world today. It's a small shift in focus that makes a huge difference in the way we experience life.

The most important thing to remember is that God loves us unconditionally and is always available to help us learn to live richer and happier lives. God finds us wherever we are. And how can this not be true since God is inside us? We have been given an open-ended invitation to be one with our Creator inside our own hearts and by acknowledging and accepting this invitation, we become new.

We can't be perfect, but we *can* learn from our mistakes. Falling down is an important part of life and it's what you learn on the ground and how you get back up that makes you who you are. We often don't have a choice about what happens in our lives, but we do have a choice about how we *respond* to what happens. In these choices, we can learn to pick up our God-given power a little bit at a time. The key is to recognize *your* moments of power and learn how to make constructive choices for yourself and for the world.

Developing a Spiritual Practice

If I do nothing else in this work, I hope to inspire you to develop a daily, living Spiritual Practice, something that brings you into a closer relationship with your Creator. In this way, a Spiritual Practice is similar to what you might call your personal relationship with God except we're going to ramp it up a bit, take it deeper, and make it more alive. We're going to practice being involved with God, daily and actively.

Your practice will not look exactly like mine because you are not me. God shows up differently in you and for you and that is exactly how it's meant to be. A personal relationship with God doesn't come from the words you read in a book, any book. It comes from the places that those words touch inside you. It comes when you show up, every day and in every way possible, and you ask to be guided. It shows up in fits and starts and in long periods when God seems to be silent. It shows up when you continue to ask how to love more. It comes when you use every experience you can get your hands on to teach yourself to better align with Spirit. It shows up every way you can handle. And sometimes it shows up in ways you think you can't handle. Yes, God really shows up.

Buddhism talks about the idea that all life is suffering. I'm not a Buddhist but for me that statement means the experience of being human (Divine Spirit in a human body) is a lot harder than being fully in Spirit. Heaven sounds better than Earth, right? A Spiritual Practice is an ongoing process that leads us toward wholeness, toward God. We might say that a Spiritual Practice creates Heaven on Earth. In this way, a Spiritual Practice is a way to relieve suffering.

One thing we must remember as we begin to have experiences that feel more like Heaven on Earth is that we are not *going* anywhere. This is not about escape. We are here now and we are meant to be here now. This is about shifting our perception so our lives become new and different — right where we are. It's about inviting Spirit into our daily lives, not hiding from our lives. The world doesn't necessarily change: *You* change — and then the world looks different.

This Earth walk is critically important to God's Plan and it's important that we show up passionately in the here and now and participate in The Plan. How do I know it's important? Because we are here. If this wasn't really important, God wouldn't have wasted time and resources creating us in the first place and he wouldn't have stayed involved as we progress. God is here because we are here and we are important to The Plan.

A note about the passage of time as you develop your Spiritual Practice: It might get "worse" before it gets better. I tell you this now because we humans tend to be really fond of instant gratification. This is not like that. This will be some of the hardest work you have ever done and it might get really tough as you go deeper inside to heal your own darkness and pain. The good news is that it will also get easier as you move forward. In the beginning I thought of it this way: "It took me thirty-some years to get this messed up. If it only takes me thirty-some years to fix it, I'm still doing OK." Many of my lessons have taken years to learn. *Years.* The good news is that it doesn't take as long to heal as it took to get messed up because now you are working with intention. Now you have a plan. Keep praying. Keep going deeper. Don't give up on your Self!

As radical as these ideas may seem at first reading, there is nothing really "new" here. I use the King James and the New Revised Standard (NRSV) versions of the Bible in my study. The words have always been there. What is new is the voice of God moving through the words and the lens through which the words are being interpreted. My aim in this writing is to move away from the emphasis on sin and unworthiness and into the promise that each and every one of us is a cherished and beautiful child of God.

If we want to get the most we can out of this life, to be truly joyful and purposeful, to help create a better world, we must learn to live from the Divine Spark, The Christ that is within us all. To live from it, we must first acknowledge that it exists. Then we can begin to act from it. It's not an easy thing to do when you're plagued by doubts and fears, when you feel so very human and fragile most of the time, or when you find yourself in a system that tells you constantly that you're a sinner. The only way to do it is to take one baby step at a time, remembering that each and every one of us is a work in progress. We are masterpieces being created every single day.

The Paradox

It has been said that the ability to live with ambiguity is a sign of spiritual maturity. This has been crucial for me to remember and it will be crucial for you to remember as you read and struggle with these concepts. Contemplation of profound and important subjects such as God and the meaning of life demands that we deal with constant ambiguity, as it necessitates bumping up against the mystery of the unknown. The paradox here is that none of us can *prove* God, but this does not mean God is not real — and it need not keep us from knowing God in our lives.

Because human beings tend to overcomplicate things unnecessarily, it can be confounding for us to rest in the gray area where we might find God's truth to be very simple. When I study and contemplate meaning in the Bible, I'm often reminded to step back from the overly analytical, grown-up person I *think* I am and see with the eyes of innocence. This simplification isn't about seeing things as black and white. It's about setting down the weapon of judgment and learning to see the beauty in everything, as a child does. This shift in perception relates to what Jesus taught about our human tendency to get stuck in all the details (i.e., the letter of the law rather than the spirit, semantics instead of the heart of the matter) and forget that God calls us, first and foremost, simply to love. Perhaps this is what Jesus meant when he said:

> Verily I say unto you, except ye be converted, and become as little children, ye shall not enter into the kingdom of heaven.[7]

My task here is made somewhat easier by the fact that my goal is not to convert anyone to a specific doctrine. I do, however, want to make reasonable and rational statements about what is, in truth, vastly unknowable. My task is more daunting because interpreting the Bible in new ways runs

---

7   Matthew 18:3

contrary to the beliefs of many people. Regardless of your religious or spiritual persuasion, you will come up against ideas and interpretations that are uncomfortable or that you have not thought about before. As you read, try not to push too hard against the details. Rather let the ideas flow through you. If it feels right for you, let the ideas settle and see how they speak to you over time. In this way you will begin to hear the voice of God moving through the words, which is much more important than the exact words I have put on the page.

We are about to take a journey through the old texts and the teachings of Jesus where I have found a truth that has largely remained hidden in plain sight. I invite you to go inside yourself and create a state of being that says "yes" to the call of your own Divinity. Tell God you're ready and ask the Spirit of unconditional love, what many call the Holy Spirit, to take root in your heart. Then as this Spirit blossoms, your hands can become tools for creating hope, joy, and peace. We can change our lives and the world. "With God all things are possible."[8] Show up. Open. Go into the silence of your own heart and invite the Divine Presence to speak to you. Then be patient and listen.

"Be still and know that I Am God."[9]

Be still and know. Be still. Be.

---

8   Matthew 19:26
9   Psalm 46:10

Setting a Foundation

Before the Beginning

You can prove almost anything you want to prove with the Bible. Then you can turn around and prove the opposite of what you already proved just by reading a different passage, changing your focus, using a different translation, or changing the way you interpret the words.

You might be wondering why God would want it this way. Perhaps it is so we have to think! We are here to experience and choose and live in the mystery of this journey. What would be the point of coming into these physical bodies if we were given all the answers to all the questions before we even got here? Whatever God is, it would be silly to define him/her/it as being so small that we humans can easily understand and define everything in the Divine Plan. This is big stuff we're talking about and the biggest piece of our assignment is just to show up and put ourselves out there. Let's face it: if we could have stayed fully Spirit and skipped this whole earthly struggle thing, we probably would have. But being here, having these human experiences, making choices, making mistakes, learning to love: these are the very reasons we are here. Life lessons are often painful, but that doesn't mean they should be denied or avoided. They are opportunities for learning and growth if we are willing to embrace them.

Growing up in a Southern Baptist church, I was taught that God was "out there," as opposed to also being "in here." I was taught that if you were good you went to Heaven and if you were bad you burned in Hell. (Unfortunately, everybody's definitions of "good" and "bad" were different, which made me a little nervous.) All that focus on "out there" and what happens after we die didn't really make sense to me and eventually I got tired of waiting for something to happen "out there" and decided to show up and participate in what is happening right here and now.

I live now with the belief that God is in everything and, most importantly, God is "in here" — inside each one of us. By making this shift in my perception, I came to realize that Heaven and Hell exist just as much here on Earth as they might in the afterlife and, in a very real way, we contribute to the creation of one or the other every day with the choices we make. For all I know my life now may be my only experience on Earth, so I choose to live by experiencing and expressing the essence of God's love — what Spiritual people call the Christ Consciousness — as much as possible. It makes me happy to live this way. Since none of us can *prove* God from this earthly existence, we won't really know the ultimate truth until we die. When I die and this body is buried in a hole in the ground, if that turns out to be the end of it, I didn't lose anything. I will have lived my life passionately, in love and in God, and that is a gracious plenty.

When Would NOW Be A Good Time?

After I had been involved in the Episcopal Church for about a year, one of my new friends, Ted, asked me a really important question: "Now that you've spent time with us, what do you see as the differences between Christians and the Spiritual Community you came from?" What follows is a synopsis of our conversation.

For me, the primary differences are "time and focus." It's not that Christians and I differ so much on what the words mean, but I believe there are things we are meant to be doing right now that Christianity talks about as being "in the future." Correct me if I'm wrong, but it seems a lot of Christians believe the Kingdom of Heaven refers to something that is going to happen at some future time. I once wrote about what Jesus might have meant when he said, "The kingdom of Heaven is at hand"[10] and I considered the hands of a human being. How far away is your hand? (Now you're supposed to put your hand right up in front of your face and see how close it is.) Are we not here

---

10   Matthew 4:17

on Earth either in Heaven or in Hell, depending on our choices? We don't have to wait for a time when blood is running in the streets; blood already runs in the streets on Earth. And Heaven already exists, too, when we choose to see it. We are here now and this is our charge: to be Christ-like, as best we can, in these human bodies. We volunteered and were chosen to come here to create in the likeness and image of God.

So now we arrive at the difference in perspective between "I'm a sinner" and "I'm a beautiful child of God." You can say both are true — and I agree. Now, which one do we focus on? At this point in the conversation, Ted even wondered aloud why he doesn't think of himself more often as a beautiful child of God. Some Christians tend to keep the focus on sin, constantly reminding themselves and everyone else how bad we are. I prefer to focus on God's love and move into the Kingdom that is here for us right now, when we choose to perceive it.

So why are people so focused on sin? Priests in the early Church wanted to bring God to the people, but they were human beings, just like us, controlled by ego to some extent like we all are. Focusing on sin and fear, hell-fire and damnation was a good way for the priests to control the people and get them to do what they wanted them to do. In the end the priests took most of the power from the people. This system proved to be rife with opportunities for ego to come in and convince the leaders they were more important than everyone else — and suddenly the end justified the means. People were told that God gave his power to only a select few and the only way someone could get to God and be saved from eternal damnation was through the Elect — and the people believed! (But oh my, the ego in that kind of thinking is staggering.) Of course, the Church also managed to spread the Word of God in the process and that is a beautiful thing. But in some ways, what the Church has done does not seem consistent with what Jesus taught.

Jesus talked about what we can do to live aligned with God's Will — and he embodied that. He demonstrated what it looks like to pick up our power. He said, "Greater things than I have done, you will do."[11] That statement is about us. Sometimes it's difficult and even scary to consider, but I believe he wanted us to do what he did: to be God in this world to the best of our ability. It's probably easier to control others with fear than with love. The problem is, you don't create full, rich, healthy people that way. You create followers. In my humble opinion, it's not enough for people to do what they do simply because they're told to do it — and it's really unhealthy for them to do things only because they're afraid not to.

So time and focus are the primary differences between my beliefs and those of Christianity. We are meant to be intimately involved in a personal relationship with God, right now, and sometimes that means refusing to let someone else scare us into agreeing with them. At my church, priests and teachers give us ideas and help us develop our relationships with God and our friends do that, too. That's what community and fellowship are all about. Unfortunately, too much of religion seems to separate people into "us and them," making "us" right and "them" wrong. Jesus didn't do that. The

---

[11] 2 John 14:12

Second Coming

spirituality I practice knows that we are all One — and Jesus teaches me how to be a vibrant part of The One every day!

God is Still Talking

In this book I used the notes from my study of the life and teachings of Jesus, and from having spent 15 years in a Spiritual Community that uses the guidance of many other great teachers as well. Yes, of course others have taught similar messages and of course we can find God everywhere we look. My Spiritual Community included recovering Christians and Catholics, people who sought the Divine in nature, Pagans, Buddhists, students of *A Course in Miracles,* and those who practiced Native American traditions. Some followed Spiritual paths I can't even name. And we all did our discovery in a sanctuary with stained-glass windows of Jesus, under a sacred dome. If you find your teacher to be of a name other than Jesus and know this to be your Creator speaking to you in a way that makes your heart sing, read on. It is not my goal to teach Christianity. My goal is to experience and teach about Christ, the Christ Consciousness, which is our birthright, given freely by God to us through grace. If sharing my story helps you find your way to the Creator, then we are both blessed by this work.

Second Coming

You may be wondering how we make a conscious connection with something so vast as the Creator of the Universe. How do we begin to hear the voice of God in our everyday lives? The best explanation I have heard is the metaphor of the voice coming out of your radio. The voice is carried on sound waves that are always present around us. However, until we turn our radio on and tune into the frequency that carries the sound, we cannot hear it.

Hearing God's Voice

I used to think those strange looks I got from people were because they thought I was nuts for believing God was talking to me. Then the men in my Bible study told me that when they first met me, the voices of doubt and fear from their own egos caused them to look at me strangely. The voice they were hearing in their minds was saying, "If God talks to her, why doesn't God talk to me?" I never realized that people felt this way when I told them about talking to God.

Ironically, the reason I didn't realize people were experiencing their own doubts and fears was due to my own ego and fear about not wanting people to think I'm crazy. We'll talk about the voice of ego later but you can see how our interpretations of others can become convoluted. Now I can see that people weren't judging me at all; they were judging themselves.

The guys in Bible study revealed even more fear: "What if I'm afraid to hear God's voice because I'm afraid I can't do what God asks of me? Or what if I don't want to do what God asks of me?" We had an amazing discussion that day.

It says in the Bible, "Those with ears, let them hear."[12] If we want to hear the voice of God, we need to tune in and open our ears, hearts, and minds. God's voice is always there, waiting patiently for us to listen — and the minute we tune in and are ready to hear, the voice is already speaking.

One obstacle that many of us face in hearing the voice of God relates to our culture: listening has become a lost art. We may have ears, but that doesn't mean we are open to hearing what is being said. We must learn to be still and focus. The statement *"Those with ears, let them hear"* or more typically in the language of King James, *"He that hath an ear, let him hear"* is made many times throughout the books of Matthew, Mark, and Luke and in the Book of Revelation. When I studied religion in college, we were taught that if the Bible says something more than once, you better pay attention! Something repeated so often indicates it is very important so maybe we had better start honing our listening skills.

One way to practice listening is to hear other people with your heart, not just your ears and mind. After all, each one of us is a house of God and another person's truth can help you get closer to your own if you really pay attention. And you can't do this with the TV on!

Hearing what comes to us from outside of ourselves is important, but it is also critically important to listen to the voice of God within yourself. I'm an extrovert and throughout my life I have done such a good job of listening to others that I have often forgotten to listen to the Divine Presence within me. This has caused me trouble

---

12   Mark 4:9 & Luke 8:8 are examples

in a couple of different ways. I have habitually given more credence to what other people think than to my own perspectives. I have also tended to give preference to the overly critical voices in my head — the ones that belong to the ego and say I'm not good enough — over the voice of Spirit, which tells me I Am precious and loved. Of course, we all have these negative voices inside of us. You know, the ones that pitch a big, loud fit, making it much harder to hear the voice of God, which often whispers to us in the silence.

Whatever voices you are giving preference to over the voice of God — be they internal or external — it is so important for each of us to learn to quiet them so we can focus on the most important one: God speaking directly to each of us. The Bible even gives us clues about what it's like to tune in to the Divine Voice:

> And thine ears shall hear a word
> behind thee, saying, This is the way,
> walk ye in it, when ye turn to the right hand,
> and when ye turn to the left.[13]

God did not stop talking 2,000 years ago. As a matter of fact, God talks to us every single day in myriad ways; we simply need to learn to pay attention. We also need to heal so we feel worthy to hear the voice of God. It's hard to be quiet and listen when our lives are in turmoil, when we feel helpless and hopeless, or when the voice of ego runs amuck.

---

13   Isaiah 30:21

What's It Really Like?

As I worked on this book, I asked people to read it and give me feedback. The comment I heard most often was, "What is it really like? Tell more stories! I need to know what it's really like!" I know hearing other people's stories is helpful, especially when we are in uncharted waters, so I'll do my best ...

So what is it like to hear God's voice? It is indescribable. It's like hearing with your body or your heart rather than hearing with your ears or your mind. I hear actual words in my head but it's as though I did not form the words with my own mind. The words seem to be fully formed inside me, in my Soul — and who really knows where the Soul is located in the body? It's everywhere, isn't it? So the words I hear are not sounds coming from the outside. It's just something I know suddenly and quietly. I feel God moving inside of me.

It's hard to describe because we are so overly attached to our minds and so overly impressed with how smart we think we are and how we have it all figured out. And then here comes God, whom we will never figure out. God says a few small "words" and suddenly your whole being fills up with an undeniable knowing that would take volumes to explain. But you don't need volumes because you just know.

I don't know why we're so afraid to say God talks to us but we all hear God in some way if we want to. We just don't admit it, lest people think we're nuts. That was one of my first steps: deciding it was OK if people thought I was a little crazy. The people who know me, know me. And they really like "my kind of crazy." And the people who judge me may always judge me. They are none of my business, bless their hearts.

Once when I was feeling particularly judged by someone, I heard God say, "So who are you going to listen to? Him or me?" It was that simple. And the choice was easy.

The Word

God's voice can also speak through the written word, becoming a living thing that interacts with the reader. Whether we're talking about the Bible or other texts dedicated to God, all can be interpreted in different ways depending on the perceptions and experiences of each reader — and all of these texts are available for us to move into and through, making them an active part of our daily lives.

I believe the Bible is the word of God and that it is meant to reach everyone, so it must speak to everyone right where they are. I'm not living 2,000 years ago in Israel. I'm here. Now. Perhaps the reason Jesus spoke in often vague and misunderstood parables is because it allows the words to speak to every reader according to the circumstances of his or her own life — 2,000 years ago, 900 years ago, now, and in the future. The Bible is still relevant and alive and if you get nothing else from my words, I hope you will pick up a Bible and find support for your life in there.

Second Coming

> **Transactional Theory of Literary Work**
>
> The idea that a text and reader interact to create meaning is not a new one. Louise M. Rosenblatt published a foundational text in 1978 that has challenged traditional ideas of interpretation in the fields of literary criticism, education, rhetoric, and others. It is called *The Reader, the Text, the Poem,* and in it Rosenblatt expounds upon the theory that there is no one "right" interpretation of any piece of writing. Depending on an individual's gender, race or ethnicity, culture, socioeconomic status, sexual orientation, life experience, and other factors, different words can take on different meanings. Of course, this does not mean that any interpretation goes: we must still be faithful to the words on the page. But many academics now subscribe to the idea that we each bring a piece of ourselves to whatever we read and no one meaning necessarily deserves preference over another.

Then there is the Living Word, which is how many people think of Jesus and what many others call the Christ Consciousness or the voice of the Holy Spirit. Jesus was a human being who lived the Word of God as an example for us to follow by showing us the Christ Consciousness — God inside the man.

Sometimes God's living word doesn't manifest as actual words, written or heard. Sometimes God prefers to come to us as a miracle or through a person who shows up as an angel, being God for us in times of need. We simply need to be open to all possibilities. God is right here, all the time, and we have been given an open invitation to be in loving relationship with our Creator.

I love how they said it once at my Episcopal church: "Are we not part of the Mystery of the Word made flesh?" Amen to that.

Inner Dance

One day when I was really struggling, I turned to God and said, "Help me!" I started writing and this is the comfort and guidance that was given to me. It doesn't really matter what my issue was on this particular day, since we all have similar struggles. I share this just as it came through to me. I hope it will speak to you as you contemplate your own dark days. As always, when we are open, God's voice speaks into the darkness and brings light.

April 2012

Something of a line has been drawn, not between the hemispheres of the brain, but between the "hemispheres" of the whole person. You know yourself to be a creature of duality, Soul and ego housed in a body. One body with two seemingly irreconcilable forces moving within. This is so and not so. The difference in the two is smaller than you might think, but the direction, the aim, of the two is different. The focus, so to speak. One, the ego, lives in fear of its own death because like the body it will, in fact, die someday, so it is constantly striving to move upward, so to speak, as if to save itself from forces that would crush it. The Soul "moves" in the other direction, constantly seeking to stay seated in the body — not because it is afraid not to but because it chooses to stay and with great joy. This is the primary difference between the two forces: One feels trapped and fights to get away from what it fears, even though it cannot exist if it "gets away" and it knows this. The other is in gratitude and service and strives only to stay. Both are necessary parts of the whole and the combination of the two energies is the essence of free will and duality.

It is impossible for these two forces not to mingle. As a matter of fact, it is necessary that they do, since this is the purpose of life: to house Spirit in a body in order to experience "the other," the thing that could not be experienced when there was only "One of Us." This is the great joy, the beautiful dance of great cooperation, played out in the Earthly arena and in Eternity. You miss the importance of this dance, since it is nothing more than your waking and your sleeping and everything that comes when you mingle together. It is like the air you breathe ... and just as important. Think about it: You take the air for granted, barely noticing the gift until the moment the gift is taken from you. Then the air is the most important thing, the only thing. Is this not the same with your life: It is ho-hum, work-a-day, up one and down the other ... so often it is "just life." Until it could end. This is the gift that death so often brings; it brings life back to the living.

Another piece you miss is that "the other" in the dance is not always the other human. Very often, most often, it is "the other" housed inside each of you. The inner dance orchestrates the outer dance. This is why when you give all your attention away

Inner Dance

to the outside of you, you miss the importance of the forming ground. The outer dance is critically important: It is the vehicle for the reason you are here, but the inner dance is the engine in the vehicle. The inner dance is the core, but the inner dance cannot happen without "the other" who pushes the buttons and changes the tires ... or not. You see how they mingle. It is always a choice.

But a fine line can be drawn — and this is the line where Peace exists. The bridge between these two aspects is thin, permeable, constantly flowing, often appearing to be non-existent, but it is there. The Peace is created by recognizing and focusing on the inner dance and allowing it to create the outer, rather than allowing the outer dance to run the show.

Remember, the ego, the outer, "the other" ... these are all words that are driven by the struggle to survive, which is important. The inner stays by choice and in Love and is, therefore, the one who brings Peace. But the inner without the outer does not exist in this world, so the outer is critically important. And so you must learn to be in this flow.

Flow is not always in one direction. If you could truly see the river, in all its molecules, you would understand flow. It is a ghost of water, a smoke. This, too, is your dance. How do you value both equally, giving one its head, but not pulling back too hard on the other? The movie said, "You can't ride two horses with one ass." This is a much more profound statement than you might imagine.

It says in the Bible that you cannot serve two Masters. In fact, you can, but it doesn't work very well and it might make you crazy. The religionists turned this statement outward, as humans are wont

Second Coming

to do, and turned it into a choice between choosing God or evil, Spirit or the earthly pleasures. This is a way to use wisdom to teach or control, giving the black and the white of it and saying that you must choose between the two. Except that, as we have seen, this is not a black-and-white existence for you. It cannot be. Not because of the outer experience, but because you must bring the outer in and the inner must go out and it must all flow together. This is what you accepted in the Garden and in that moment, the "experiment" went from junior high science, where "this always reacts like that," to ... well ... Albert can explain that to you. He understands it better from here. (Smile.)

It's complicated. And it doesn't get less complicated quickly or without much Grace and effort. See, we did it again ... Grace and effort ... Spirit and body/ego. It doesn't go away — and only coming to Peace makes it easier. You underestimated the power of your choice when you settled on the words "Synergy Alliance." This describes the entire dance of human and Spirit.

Now you have experienced moments on this bridge of Peace we have described. The inner and the outer are both present. You are one who has worked to keep your focus on Spirit for a very long time and yet, the ego still vies for position and then you suffer again. Recently you have experienced a new peacefulness with "the line" between the two. You can very accurately call this the veil between the worlds, because both of "the worlds" exist within you. This is, "As above so below," but humans so often discount themselves so much that they forget they are the most critical part of the Grand Design.

"How can this be? I'm flawed, I'm nothing," you say. And we say, you are not flawed. You are set up in a difficult and important process for the purpose of experiencing a critical level of development ... to love "The Other" both inside and out. And you, Lily, are finally learning that when you didn't love the inner, the outer was much more painful.

You are in the next step of Self Love: Having learned the new skill, you are now experiencing what happens when Self Love, which is for the Whole of the dance, is in charge. In case you are wondering (and we know you are!) the shift happened for you in the moment you realized that "Love God, Love your neighbor, and love yourself" are all the same thing. You had worked that verse for a lifetime (actually more) and still, in that moment, you came to a new awakening ... the profound truth that says, "In Spirit, all are The One." Period. Before this moment you simply had to believe that God brought all the children home because you were so afraid you were the one who would be left behind, due to a lack of merit. And so your strivings were still based in fear. Now you know.

And then you all volunteered and were chosen to come here and experience what it was like to look at The One, to look at your self and your Self, "on the outside." To see what you knew "on the inside" as One Being, what you now call God, in the mirror of many.

Agendas

Hidden and Otherwise

We all have agendas. An agenda is simply a list of things to do or a plan for how you will do things in life. Of course, I want to live my life the way I choose to live it and you want to do the same in your life. The problem arises when there is a "hidden agenda." Hidden agendas sometimes show up when we try to make other people do things the way *we* want them to be done, without informing the other person that we have put ourselves in charge of *their* lives. Or, in terms of spiritual healing, you might even hide your agenda from yourself.

I try to keep my agendas open and as transparent as possible. While this is nice for other people, since it's honest and aboveboard, the primary reason I like openness and clarity about my agenda is because *it keeps me honest with myself.* This is very important when we talk about healing our lives. In my inner circle of Spiritual friends, we do a lot of healing around the experience of lying to ourselves. We call this part of the work,

"I'm a Liar." It involves catching yourself in the act of pretending one thing and doing another and it is not the most fun part of the curriculum of life. When we are afraid to look at a flaw or a fear in our own lives and we haven't healed it yet, very often it keeps showing up in our actions toward ourselves and other people. These lies we tell ourselves continue to show up until we heal them. Without such intervention, they can create patterns of negative behavior that last throughout our lives.

We hide things from ourselves all the time and then we ignore what we know is seething underneath. It is not healing to simply stuff our doubts and fears down deep and pretend they no longer exist. That is called denial and it makes us sick and mean. From a Christian perspective, we could say that unhealed wounds, doubts, and fears are what cause us to sin. (We'll talk more about sin later.) Spiritual healing lifts our inner conflicts, pain, wounds, doubts, and fears up to the light of God. As people in 12-step programs say, "When we stuff our feelings, they are buried alive." Lies we tell ourselves are at the core of the lies we tell other people, so this kind of healing is not just a gift to ourselves; this part helps change the world.

The Biggest Lies

The biggest lies are the ones we tell ourselves and since we can only be as honest with other people as we are with ourselves, it's important to uncover the ways in which we lie to ourselves. For example, we might lie to ourselves when we feel ashamed, afraid, or unworthy. We want to do better and we want to be accepted by others, so we lie to make ourselves feel better about what hurts.

Agendas

When it comes to my relationship with God and what you are reading in this book, my agenda says things like: God really does love us just as we are — and one of the most important reasons we are here is simply to learn from the experience of being human. Redemption speaks to the idea that God wants to help us heal. I do not believe that God says, "Yes, I created you and I love you unconditionally *but ...*" Unconditional means there are no "buts!" God just loves us.

The definition of God's Grace says that we do not have to do anything to receive it. Grace is a gift freely given by God to us. Some people say we do not *deserve* God's grace, but by definition, Grace simply says we do not have to *do* anything to earn it. That's not the same as saying we don't deserve it. We were put here in this free will system to make choices and learn, and we will naturally make mistakes. God loves us anyway. Even when we fall down God simply wants us to learn to get back up again.

Think about the children in your own life: When they make mistakes, you don't stop loving them. Even though you do not always like what they do, you still love them and you teach them how to make better choices. If we are capable of loving through the mistakes, it follows that God is at least as capable as we are.

When I think of God as a parent, I sometimes wonder which of my drawings God has on the refrigerator?

> ### The Unconditional Love of God, The Father
>
> When my son Scott read my manuscript, he said, "Mom, it sometimes amazes me how vastly separate the concepts of unconditional love and God are in some peoples' minds. I think this is what keeps a great many people away from organized religion, as they so often present the image that God might love us a little bit ... but mostly he's just pissed. And I like that you talk about the relationship between children and their parents. We often talk about God as a "Father" but by the definition of God that some religions come up with, in all honesty, God would be a terrible father!"
>
> Scott also commented on the integration of Spiritual and Christian ideas, saying it gives people the opportunity to open to new interpretations of their own ideas as well as ideas from the "other side" that they might have otherwise rejected. In this way, sharing our stories and speaking our truth to one another gives us all permission to explore and it allows us to enhance one another's spiritual journey.

When we go into the Bible with personal agendas — our plans for life and how we perceive reality — we find what we look for. My old friend and sparring partner, who saw himself as completely unworthy of God's love, interpreted everything in the Bible as a confirmation of his belief.

I deliberately look for God's love. That is my agenda. I believe God loves me and I look for ways to prove it. When some people go into the Bible, they expect to find God's condemnation because they remind themselves constantly of their belief that defines God in this way. They were taught that this is how people should experience God. We each find what we look for. That is why I can read the same Bible verse as someone else and come away with a different interpretation. I expect to find Love, so I do. If you expect to find judgment and sin, shame, and condemnation, you will find that as well.

"Don't Look Where You Don't Want to Go."

Looking where we don't want to go can get us into trouble. This happens in our daily lives. People often get hit by cars while walking on the side of the road simply because drivers keep looking at them and then run right into them. We are literally, and sometimes physically, motivated to move in the direction of our focus.

Some Spiritual people refer to this concept as, "We find what we look for." That is why a focus on healing is important if we want to experience the peace of God. Philippians 4:7 says, "The peace of God, which passes all understanding, shall keep your hearts and minds through Christ Jesus." God's peace is found in our hearts. So if God's peace and love is what we want, we need to look for it and be open to it. We need to be in our hearts.

Focusing primarily on sin is only one side of the coin. I keep my focus on healing, which is the other side of the same coin. This shift in focus from fear to love has led me to peace.

My Agenda

In my writing, you won't read about how bad we are. I find that focus to be counter-productive. Plus I think we do a pretty good job of reminding ourselves how bad we are and how much we've screwed up without someone else bringing it up. My relationship with my Creator has much more to do with getting better and being happier. Mine is a redeeming God, not a punishing God, so you will learn how God lifts me up and shows me how to make better choices instead of how God beats me down about something I did wrong. And I don't think much about "sin." Not because I don't do the things that people call sin; I do. But I think a lot more about healing, rising up, doing better, being fuller and richer in my life. For me, this is all about being loved by God, just as I am.

I find it interesting that some of the more fundamentalist interpretations of Christianity constantly remind us that we cannot do enough good works to get into heaven — that God's grace is the only way to be saved. However, these same folks will go on and on about what sinners we are, which is all about the things we do. Correct me if I'm wrong, but isn't this a contradiction we cannot win? We don't get any credit for doing good things, but we get punished for doing bad things. Seriously?

These same people would criticize my agenda and point out that all I'm doing here is cherry picking the parts about love and peace and uplifting Spirit while downplaying the parts about shame, guilt, and sin. They are absolutely right! That is exactly what I'm doing and I feel Jesus calling me to do it. I do exactly what the fundamentalists do except I do it in the other direction. It is no more wrong to highlight just the "love stuff" than it is to preach only about sin and shame. I have learned to focus on how amazing and loved and powerful we can be when we finally stop beating ourselves to death with shame-filled interpretations of the Bible and start listening to that still, small voice of God saying, "See what real love can do. Try this."

The healing work I do extends beyond reading the Bible and praying for help. My Spiritual Practice includes daily and continuous application of a spiritually based form of conflict resolution. I don't do this work because it is all happy and easy. Healing is the hardest work I've ever done in my life. When you say, "Speak to me, Lord, and show me the way to be better in this life," God shines a very bright light and illuminates every dark corner you have — and you are compelled by the Divine to go there and see your own darkness in order to heal it. This part could easily be called, "Congratulations, you're dying," because we must die to the old self in order to be born to the new Self. I do my healing work because it makes my life better. I'm no different than anyone else in this world who needs to heal.

My Agenda

I write about it because it fulfills my personal calling from God. The concepts in this book are what I believe Jesus was trying to get us to understand all along. This is what the Second Coming of Christ is all about — and we need to stop waiting for someone else to do it for us. It is time. The Kingdom of Heaven is at hand and if we're too busy beating ourselves up to notice, then we will not experience it.

What's It Really Like – What Do I Do?

People ask me all the time, "But what can I do to have this relationship with God? Tell me what to do and I'll do it." I cannot tell you what to do to make this work, but I will share what God said when I asked the same question: "Stop worrying about what you're doing and just keep doing it."

There's a reason it's called a practice. You do it every day. You practice. It's no different than learning to play the piano or tennis. The more you practice, the easier it gets. Practice means focusing on the basics, over and over again. Rest assured that the best athletes in the world do not suddenly proclaim one day, "OK, I'm good enough now. I think I'll stop practicing." They practice every day. If you want to be a great basketball player, you shoot millions of baskets. And the essence is the same in your spiritual practice. If you want to have a great relationship with God, show up every day and pay attention to all of the signs and awakenings that life delivers to you to help you learn. The more you pay attention, the more you realize you are being offered millions of opportunities to do just that. Open your heart and discover the messages. Practice.

Jesus, The Christ and Us

Created in the Image of God

In Genesis, God says:

> Let us make humankind in our image.[14]

What does that really mean? Since God doesn't have a physical body except when incarnate, it wouldn't make sense that this statement is about *our* bodies. But it says *image* and an image is about what something looks like, right? Not necessarily. Certainly this is one definition of *image*. Our culture is very focused on the visual: We "see" what someone is saying rather than hearing it, we "watch" television and movies even though these mediums involve more than just the sense of sight, and our physical bodies are certainly easier to "see" than our Spirits. So it makes sense that this is the definition of *image* that we focus on. However, if we take a look at other definitions, we learn that *image* can refer to more than just physical appearance. According to the dictionary, an image can also be *a mental representation, idea, or conception; a counterpart or copy; and even an*

---

14 Genesis 1:26

embodiment or type.[15] So, depending upon which definition is privileged, this verse can actually be interpreted to mean that humankind was made as the idea, counterpart, or even the embodiment of God.

Taken this way, it is easier to hear the Bible speaking of the Divine Spirit or Soul, which *animates* the physical body and without which the physical body ceases to live. Being created in the Image of God then means that our essential nature, our core, is Divine Spirit. It is from this place of Spirit that we must begin our conversation about awakening The Christ within. We are the embodiment of God's Spirit.

This piece of information is huge and without this first step it is difficult to take this journey with new eyes and open ears. So what do we do with this amazing information? We begin to embody it. Or we deny it. We have the choice to do either — and the choice we make will determine our next steps in life with respect to who we truly are and how we act in the world. Whether we choose to deny our Divine core — or to live from it — is a choice we make every day. Sometimes it is not easy to accept that we have God inside us; on the tough days, it is nearly impossible. This is the story of what it means to be a human being.

Accepting this truth and moving toward its fulfillment has been the greatest journey of my life. Learning that human beings are made of God is a tremendous responsibility, because once you know this and believe it, then you must learn to live from that place of Divinity and give up your doubts and fears — and your excuses. You must learn to stop complaining, stop pointing fingers at other people, and get up off the couch and do

---

15 dictionary.com

something to make a difference in your life — and in the world. Take responsibility for your own life and figure out where you have power to change it instead of doing what we've all been taught to do in this culture, which is to blame someone else for what we don't like.

It's true that a multitude of things are out of your control. You were born into a world of many injustices and other people make choices that affect you every day without consulting you about them. However, feeling like a victim doesn't make anything better. Once you own the power of God that is inside you, you'll be better able to see where you have power in your daily life. This may be as simple as a shift in focus or a decision to try something new, or it may be as grand as the renouncement of a toxic relationship or the experience of a daring leap of faith. The key is to realize that in virtually every situation, there is something you can do to impact the status quo.

I once spoke on "Your Relationship to ..." at my Spiritual Community. I talked about our experiences in life and how we get to choose our relationship to the things that happen. Think of it this way: There is "the thing" (situation, person, experience) and then there is *your relationship to* "the thing." You may not be able to change "the thing" in any given situation, but you always have the power to change *your relationship to it* by shifting your perception and changing your attitude. This is what it means to pick up our power and I cite examples throughout this book so you see what this shift looks like in real life. The details may vary from day to day, but it is all about aligning to Divine Will rather than aligning with ego and its effort to survive in this world. It comes down to making choices that are for the highest good of everything concerned. This takes practice, because our choices need to be Self Loving and in service to the greater good simultaneously. That's why the choices are not always easy. We may have to constantly remind ourselves that we are Divine, and so is everyone else. The key is to align to Divinity and keep balance as much as we can. It means we learn to view ourselves and others as expressions of God on Earth — and then act accordingly.

A good guide on how to act from our Highest Self is to follow a piece of scripture that has come to be known as *The Golden Rule: "Do unto others as you would have them do unto you."*[16] This tenet illustrates why Self Love is so important to our alignment with Divine Will. It presupposes that we deserve to be treated well, that we want good and loving things done to us. The key is believing yourself worthy of good and loving things first. Then you can go out and *"do unto others."* We are not meant to stand by and let ourselves be treated badly and believe that we deserve bad treatment. When we do this, we cultivate an inner environment that expects bad treatment — and this affects how we act in the world. When we recognize our own Divinity and that of everyone else, we know ourselves to be worthy of loving kindness and this makes it easier to act out of loving kindness in the world. This is what it means to walk in this world as the image or embodiment of God.

Jesus taught that it is easy to love those who love us back, but He also said we are called to love our enemies. At my church we pray to be able to love "those who are difficult to love." It takes inner

---

16   Luke 6:31

strength and Divine guidance to have the ability to turn the other cheek when someone is hurtful to us — not because we think we deserve to be hurt but because we can see a higher way. To refuse to strike back when someone slaps us is an act of Grace and it shows us that we are in touch with Spirit instead of reacting from ego. Conversely, we have to learn, through Self Love, not to stand there and let someone continue to slap us. Sometimes we must love ourselves enough to walk away from a situation or relationship that continues to hurt.

To Pick Up Our Power

How might this look in a typical day? We have all had an experience of someone we deeply care for being really hurtful to us. When we know people well, we usually know enough about them to be hurtful, which is why our closest relationships can be the most difficult (think: family of origin, romantic partners, our children, etc.). It is also why our closest relationships can be the most fruitful in terms of healing our lives. We must remember that we always have a choice in how we respond. By doing our own healing work, we are better able to realize that people are in pain or acting out of fear when they exhibit negative behavior. I remind myself, "This is what I look like when I'm in pain, too." Another way to think of it is, "Ah, so this is what God in a body looks like on a really bad day!"

It is important not to take what other people do and say personally, since their behavior often has nothing to do with you at all. One of the most important lessons I have learned in dealing with other people's behavior is to consider, "Maybe this is not about me." I know it sounds simple but this was a big step for me because I have always had a tendency to blame myself when other people act out negatively toward me.

Second Coming

To Pick Up Our Power

Recently a man I had been dating squished me like a bug. Our budding romance had taken him to a deeply emotional place and it freaked him out. He got scared and did what many of us do: he projected his fear onto me. It was one of those situations in which there was no room for conversation. I knew I had the choice to react and be ugly back to him, or not. I chose compassion. I said a blessing and I walked away. Yes, it hurt. It still hurts, but it wasn't going to hurt less if I was hurtful back to him.

My daughter, Katie, a singer/song writer, wrote a wonderful song called "Wounded Bird." It's about how we act out our inner pain through the people around us. My favorite verse says, "Hating her won't heal the broken things inside you." We've all done it: been ugly to someone else because we were hurting. The problem is that it doesn't make our hurt go away and by acting out hatefully toward someone else, we have effectively doubled the negative energy of the situation. Not smart or productive.

It is also helpful to remember that judgment and forgiveness create a circle. Being kind to others helps us be kinder to ourselves.

Another great question we can ask ourselves when we have difficult encounters is ... Do you want to be right or do you want to have Peace?

For many people, their first response would be, "I wanna be right!" But when we step back and think about it, don't we really want more peaceful lives? A man recently yelled at me for several minutes at the gas station because my car was a bit too far over and he couldn't drive through. I apologized many times and acknowledged that I had screwed up. I was as sweet as I could be but he would not stop yelling. In those moments, I had a choice: put on my boxing gloves, step into the ring and fight with him, or stay calm and centered. Knowing that I wanted peace in my life, I was able to stay calm. I realized this man was either having a really bad day or worse — perhaps he was always angry like this. Either way, I chose to feel compassion for him and his misery, which was manifesting as miserable behavior. It didn't make him stop yelling at me but I felt a lot better having chosen peace for myself and extending peace to him. (And yes, when it was all over, I cried like a baby all the way home because it was really awful to be screamed at like that.)

I once had a huge fight with my friend Barbara, entirely via email. (From this experience came my declaration, "Email is a sure road to hell!" Do yourself a favor and don't ever have important conversations through email. You cannot see the other person's body language or hear their voice intonation so your ego can twist things into dark and scary places.) Barbara and I fought back and forth for a solid week. In the end I had a stack of paper almost an inch thick. I know this because I printed out all the emails and re-experienced them over and over throughout the fight. (Trying to be right? You bet!) Throughout that week I kept seeking reinforcement from our mutual friend Teresa, saying over and over again, "But it just doesn't make sense! I keep telling her that I agree with her and she just won't let it go." (Of course I wasn't letting it go either but since I was so sure I was right, how could I?) Finally Teresa said something that has stuck with me all these years, "Honey, sometimes it just doesn't make any sense and you just have to let it go." This was a new concept for me: I could just stop and just let it be.

I don't remember who finally picked up the phone and called the other, but as soon as the phone connection was made, Barbara and I both burst into laughter. It only took us a solid week and about a ream of paper to realize that the details weren't as important as our friendship and our inner peace. The gift of, "Sometimes it doesn't make sense and you just have to let it go," has served me well for the 15 years since that experience.

Journey Toward Wholeness

My own journey toward wholeness started through a paradigm shift with this statement:

> I Am Divine. I Am also human. I hold the key.[17]

Once I began my spiritual awakening, it was as though I had those words on a little post-it note pasted right between my eyes where I could not escape back into the denial that said, "No, I'm just a flawed human being who cannot make any real, lasting difference in this world, so why bother trying?" Now, mind you, I actually am a flawed human being, but focusing on my flaws never did anything other than cause me to feel worse and be less proactive in my life. Once God started talking to me — teaching me how to reach for my Divine potential — everything changed. I began to keep my chin up, take pride in my accomplishments, and give thanks to God for everything in my life rather than focusing on what wasn't ideal and bemoaning my circumstances. Lo and behold, I was happier.

---

17   Synergy Alliance

So, when we are ready to accept this, how do we take those first steps in understanding how to make the most of this experience on Earth? One of the sayings that seems to help a lot of people was given to us by Father Pierre Teilhard de Chardin:

> "We are not human beings having a spiritual experience.
> We are spiritual beings having a human experience."

The difference in these two perspectives takes us right to the word *eternal*. The physical human body is temporary and the Spiritual Being is eternal. The Bible says it like this:

> "While we look not at the things which are seen,
> but at the things which are not seen:
> for the things which are seen are temporal;
> but the things which are not seen are eternal."[18]

> "Labour not for the meat which perishes,
> but for that meat which endures
> unto everlasting life."[19]

Call Your Father

Jesus "called home" a lot because he knew his Father was wise and strong and would always love and support him no matter what. We need to remember to call home, too.

---

18   2 Corinthians 4:18
19   John 6:27

We may talk about eternity and the idea that the soul is eternal, but how many of us actually identify with our Spirit? How many of us identify with our eternal soul as we begin each day and make decisions moving forward? Jesus did. I suggest that this was the primary difference between Jesus and the rest of humanity. He started each day, each moment, knowing he was made of God. He didn't often succumb to human temptations of doubt and fear like we often do and he didn't invest a lot of energy in the concerns of this temporary experience on Earth. Jesus knew he was eternally Divine. He also knew he was temporarily human. He knew precisely what the key was and what he was called to do: pick up his Power and stay aligned with Spirit.

This is why Jesus is my teacher, my example, and my friend. I believe his purpose was to show us how to live deeper, happier lives — God-filled lives. I don't think his primary reason for coming here was so we would all bow down and worship him and then turn around and judge our neighbors, hate our own lives, and live in hell on Earth. That invalidates what Jesus taught. By using the Bible and the teachings of Jesus, we can learn to live from a place of Spirit, just as he taught us to do.

You might be thinking, "How can we possibly use Jesus as our example, since we cannot live as he did: perfect, sinless, full of God?" Perhaps you're right and we can't be perfect like Jesus. But we have a much better chance of achieving a goal if we believe we can than if we believe we can't.

Consider this: Perhaps the whole point is about the journey and what we learn in striving to meet this goal. What would be the point of our human existence if we already had everything figured out?

The struggle is such a big part of how we learn. What have we got to lose by trying to follow the example of Jesus and by recognizing The Christ in ourselves and others? It certainly can't make things *worse!*

The following selection from Philippians is one of my favorite passages in the Bible. It gives us a clear description of how we can emulate Jesus, and why we might want to:

> Let this mind be in you, which was also
> in Christ Jesus who being in the form
> of God, thought it not robbery to be equal
> with God but made himself of no reputation,
> and took upon him the form of a servant,
> and was made in the likeness of men.
> And being found in fashion as a man,
> he humbled himself, and became obedient
> unto death, even the death of the cross.[20]

Jesus knew himself to be *"in the form of God."* The Latin word for *form* is *forma,* which literally means "shape," but it also can refer more abstractly to a "manner or type."[21] So in the abstract sense, *"in the form of God"* means Jesus was of the same type as God. The footnote on *form* in my King James Bible goes on to say that Jesus Christ "was completely God and truly man. To deny either the deity or humanity of Christ requires denying the other." Using another definition of form, *the essence of something as distinguished from its matter,*[22] means Jesus was made in the manner of God and is the same nature and essence as God.

---

20   Philippians 2:5-8
21   Notre Dame's online Latin Dictionary
22   American Heritage Dictionary

This relates to what we read in Genesis 1:26 about humankind being created in the image of God and it supports the idea that the Divine Spirit or Soul animates the physical body, making us both Divine and human. Jesus knew that even though his physical body separated him from God in one way, he was still made of God at his core. Because Jesus knew himself to be *"in the form of God,"* it makes sense that he *"thought it not robbery to be equal with God."* He knew himself to be made of God.

Many people agree with these ideas, but at the same time they do not believe this means that, like Jesus, every human is made from the essence of God at his/her core. However, when we read the passage from Philippians, it explicitly says we are to *"Let this mind be in you, which was also in Christ Jesus."* The word *mind,* used in this way, refers to "a way of thinking and feeling; a state of awareness or remembrance; or an opinion, view, or sentiment."[23] So, to let this way of thinking, this state of awareness, be in each of us as it was in Jesus, we must do as he did and realize that we too are made of God — *"equal with God"* in terms of our Divinity. Yes, our physical bodies appear to separate us from God — and we are the created, not the Creator — but we cannot discount our divinity in light of our humanity. Jesus embraced both fully and so must we.

According to notes in my King James Bible, *"made himself of no reputation"* means Jesus emptied himself: "The *kenosis* (emptying) during Christ's incarnation does not mean that He

---

23   dictionary.com

surrendered any attributes of deity, but that He took on the limitations of humanity. This involved the veiling of His pre-incarnate glory and the voluntary nonuse of some of His divine prerogatives during the time He was on earth." In other words, Jesus became human like us, but he didn't forget he was also made of God.

> ### To Empty Yourself
>
> Since learning the meaning of kenosis, the idea of "emptying" has become an important part of my healing practice. I strive to let go of some of the "limitations of humanity" in favor of embracing my own Divinity more fully. When we heal, we expose our broken places to the healing power of God's love. We give them up, so to speak. Letting go of the old wounds, the harmful thoughts, and the toxic feelings opens up a space inside of us that can then be filled with Divine Light.
>
> Spiritual people often talk about deliberately creating a space inside themselves (or in their lives) as a means of opening to new manifestation, replacing the old (and no longer needed) with new gifts from the Universe or God.

Jesus also "made himself of no reputation" by coming into the world as the child of a poor carpenter and his young wife. He chose not to come as a king, but rather as a man of no special earthly status. It might have been easier to convince people of his message if he had chosen to come as the heir to some mighty ruler, but perhaps he came as he did so that he would be viewed and treated as a peer to the everyman, rather than someone placed on a pedestal by the masses.

Likewise, God could have chosen to interact with humanity in a non-human form, appearing as an angel, a burning bush, or a disembodied voice from heaven. Instead, Jesus *"was made in the likeness of men,"* aware that he was made of God but still choosing to take on human form in order to teach us. What better way to show humanity that we could be like him, embracing our Divinity while in human form, just as he did?

"Let this mind be in you, which was also in Christ Jesus" is absolutely about all of us. We are here to awaken to The Christ inside and to be as Jesus was, fully aware of both his Divinity and his humanity. It is time for us to accept our power and begin to live as Jesus taught us to live. This is how the Second Coming will differ from the first.

We have nothing to lose by trying to emulate Jesus except maybe our doubts, fears, and shame. It's a choice. It's a small shift in perception that I think of in this way: "God really loves me and wants me to live a full, rich life, and God will help me do that. All I need to do is let the awareness of my own Divinity fill me up, just as Jesus did, and begin to move from that place. Then, over time, I will let go of my human doubts and fears, one baby step at a time, and get my ego and my free will in line with my Spirit. All I need to do is intend to live as Jesus did. He showed us what is possible. I am Divine. I am also human. I hold the key."

The Most Important Thing

Leaders of the Jewish community, considering the hundreds of commandments included in the Torah, came to Jesus and asked, "Master, which is the greatest commandment in the Law?"[24] He said,

> Love the Lord your God with
> all your heart and with all your soul
> and with all your mind. This is the first
> and greatest commandment.
>
> And the second is like it:
> Love your neighbor as yourself.
> On these two commandments hang
> all the law and the prophets.[25]

Isn't it interesting that Jesus did *not* reply, "You must worship me." As a matter of fact, he *never* said we should worship him. He also did not say, "You must accept Jesus Christ as your personal savior and you must think that everyone else should, too."

---

24   Matthew 22:36
25   Matthew 22:37-40

Second Coming

It's interesting because in that moment Jesus had the perfect opportunity to tell us just that — if that had been the most important thing for us to do in our lives. He could have said we needed to declare ourselves Christians, worship him according to a prescribed method, and get everyone else to do the same. What did Jesus actually say about that? Agreeing to an intellectual set of teachings, created by a self-declared elect group of people, was one of the things Jesus taught us *not* to do. He simply said, "Learn to love."

It is critical that each of us learn and remember the message that Jesus repeated more often than any other: You *can* live your life based on love. We are not supposed to love God simply because someone else tells us to do it or because we're afraid not to. Instead, he calls each of us into a one-on-one relationship. Yes, you might also experience this relationship in community with others and that is a beautiful thing. But remember — your relationship with God is personal. Community is meant to enhance that relationship, not define it.

Now let's look in depth at the commandment that Jesus said is the most important thing for us to do:

> Love the Lord your God with all your heart
> and with all your soul and with all your mind.
> This is the first and greatest commandment.
>
> And the second is like it:
> Love your neighbor as yourself.

Christianity has always had a firm hold on the first of the commandments on love. Love God. Of course. The first part of the second commandment — love your neighbor — is also a fundamental teaching in Christianity, although many followers struggle to match their actions to this ideal. Unfortunately, Christianity often seems to overlook the last two words of the second commandment: *"as yourself."* This is a critical distinction — and this statement can be interpreted in different ways. It can mean, "Love your neighbor as much as you love yourself," or it can mean, "Love both your neighbor *and* yourself." The important thing is that Jesus taught that we need to learn to love ourselves and to do that, we must learn to find ourselves worthy of love. In my experience, our capacity for Self Love affects our capacity for everything we do in life.

I have often wondered why Christianity seems to ignore the part of the message about loving yourself. I have a friend who, as a child, was never even taught the last two words at the end of the commandment. She was taught that the Bible said only, *"Love your neighbor."* Some even suggest that you should love other people with little or no concern or love for yourself. In this interpretation, loving yourself is considered *selfish*. But this belief contradicts the words of Christ. It also assumes that love is finite — that there is only so much of it to go around. The fear is that if we "waste" too much love on ourselves then we won't have any left to give to anyone else. In my experience, pure love begets more love. When you truly love and accept yourself, it creates a feeling of love that cannot be contained — and it overflows into your relationships and out to the world.

The truth is, you *have* to learn to love yourself to truly love your neighbor because you can't give what you don't have. You can only share what you have. A good analogy is when passengers are given safety instructions before every flight. We've all been told that in case of an emergency, put your own oxygen mask on before assisting others. It makes sense, right? If you pass out from a lack of oxygen, how are you going to help anyone else? Likewise, if you self-destruct from lack of Self Love, you won't be able to love those around you. In fact, loving other people is next to impossible if you don't love yourself. If I believe I'm worth nothing, nothing is all I have to give to you.

Let's look at it another way: Jesus said that the greatest commandment was to, *"Love the Lord your God with all your heart and with all your soul and with all your mind,"* and then he said the second commandment is just "like" the first one. Thus, these two commandments are about the same thing. That makes sense when you remember that each of us was created in the image of God. One of the most important things Jesus tried to teach us was the idea that loving yourself goes right along with loving God. How can you love God fully if you are unable to love yourself? And how can it be wrong to love yourself when you were created by God, made in the image of God, and loved by the God that created you?

Are you starting to feel how it all flows together? When you truly know yourself to be of God, then you know others to be of God as well. Loving God, loving your neighbor, and loving yourself all become one in the same. By doing one, you can't help but do all three. Yes, the most important thing is to love God and we now know that this includes both God, the Creator, and the Spirit of God, which is innate within each one of us. So, in a very real way, loving God already includes loving all of humankind, since the Spirit of God is at the core of every human being.

Perhaps Jesus could have conveyed his message more concisely by simply saying, "Love God in all forms." But he made a special effort to emphasize that the second part of the commandment was just like the first. This tells us that the human side of the equation — loving ourselves and one another — is so important that it deserves special attention. It also suggests that Jesus knew it would be tempting for us to forget or ignore ourselves and he didn't want us to do that. Until we learn to love ourselves, we will continue to put obstacles between ourselves and others, and therefore between ourselves and God.

Why Did The Messiah Come?

In the Old Testament, God said he would send a Messiah, a Deliverer. When Jesus came, he said he came to fulfill the Law and the Prophets, to accomplish what God had said. Jesus consistently reminded people, especially the religious leaders, that they were living under the Law, but they had lost the Spirit of the Law. Then he said this: To live in fulfillment of the Law, we must learn to love — love God, love our neighbor, and love ourselves.

Here's what was even more important than what Jesus said: his actions matched his words. He lived his life to teach us what miraculous things love can do and show us how to love as God loves, no matter how fragile and flawed we may feel. He came and not only delivered his message but showed us how to live in fulfillment of that message.

However, when Jesus came, many people were disappointed. They thought the Messiah would be a military leader who would save them from the suffering in their lives, perhaps by conquering all of their enemies. They didn't understand then, just as we often misunderstand now, that Jesus didn't come to save us *from* our lives; he came to save us *in* our lives. He asked us to be of "like-mind"[26] and follow the ways he taught us to live. When we do this, we are saved *in* our lives and do not need to be saved *from* our lives. This salvation is not just one moment of transformation; it is an ongoing process — from the beginning to the end of our human lives. Jesus came to show us that we can save ourselves and therefore be saved by following his teachings.

It Is Finished

People who lived at the same time as Jesus made sacrificial animal offerings to God, so it makes sense that the physical sacrifice of a human would symbolize the ultimate sacrifice for the remission of sins. Remember, Jesus came to fulfill the Law and the Prophets and by his life and his death, he did that. But there is much more to the story. The life and death of Jesus fulfilled, or completed, the old way of living under the law and he left a new way in its place: Learn to Love. The Bible says this about living in this new way:

> If it is the adherents of the law who are to be the heirs, faith is null and the promise is void.[27]

This verse tells us that we are no longer meant to live only by the law because the old law was fulfilled by the life and death of Jesus. Further, for those who continue to live only by the law, rather

26   Philippians 2:2
27   Romans 4:14

than by the fulfillment of the Spirit, faith has no place and the promises of God, now presented in a new way through Jesus, are void. In other words, living by the law alone is the way of the past and if we want to follow Jesus, we are to start living in Christ. Perhaps this is what Jesus meant, right before he died, when he said, *"It is finished."*[28]

When we are focused on the old ways — the details, the endless conversation about what sinners we are, and how other people need to "do God" the way *we* think is best — we are not in faith, not in Christ, and the promises from God are, thereby, made void. The next verse illustrates this further:

> For the law brings wrath; but where there is no law, neither is there violation.[29]

This verse tells us that when we give up the old way of living only by the law and start living in Christ and in love, there can be no violation, since the law is no longer in effect. We can't violate that which no longer exists. In this way, the life and death of Jesus ended our ability to be in violation and thereby he did, in fact, take away the sin of the world. Now that it has been taken away, it would be nice if *we* would all let it go.

He Takes Away the Sin of the World

Someone once pointed out to me that the phrase *"takes away"* is a present-tense statement. It's about being active in our relationship with Christ;

---

28   John 19:30
29   Romans 4:15

it's about a relationship that is alive and organic. It drives home the point that salvation for Christians — and Healing for Spiritual People — is a lifelong process in which we participate. Looking at it this way, *"He takes away the sin of the world"*[30] is not a statement only about what Jesus did; it is a statement about what Christ *does*. It is about what can happen every day when we let The Christ move in our lives.

Jesus even calls us to love our enemies. Obviously, all of this is a tall order. I don't know about you, but I have days when I cannot even love the people who mean the most to me, much less love myself — and on those days, loving my enemy is impossible. Actually, as I write this, I realize the whole truth: on my worst days, I'm my own worst enemy, which is precisely why I can't love anyone else! When we hurt inside, we tend to lash out and hurt others around us. People hurt because people hurt; people hurt each other and themselves because they are hurting inside.

---

30 John 1:29

What's It Really Like To Love Our Enemies?

When I first met my friend Jason, I did not like him even a little bit! He pushed every button I had about religion and I thought he was just one more fundamentalist, come to beat me with a Bible. Jason and I are different in a lot of ways when it comes to our relationship with God. I didn't know him well enough to realize that he always makes "that face" when he is concentrating. I figured he looked at me like that because he thought I was ridiculous. (Do you hear my fearful and easily bruised ego there?) One of our early conversations went like this:

"So, you talk to God?"

I said, "Yes."

"And you believe God talks back?"

"Yes."

Then he said, with "that face" that made me feel judged, even though I had no idea whether he was judging me or not, "Then why do you need all this?" (He was referring to our Sunday night Bible study and all the other things I do in my spiritual life.)

I said, "Because I'm still *very* human!"

Early on, I felt judged by Jason and my ego's reaction was to make him wrong, hoping I could stop feeling wrong. I remember the moment when I stopped feeling afraid of him. I heard God's voice say, "So, his opinion of your relationship with me is more important to you than your own opinion of your relationship with me?" Ah Ha! I was letting another human being define my relationship ... again! In that instant, I got my power back and I could stop being mad at Jason.

He and I are good friends now and we've spent many hours in deep conversation and shared contemplation about God. About a year into our friendship, in words so similar to that earlier conversation it made me think he was just teasing me, he said, "So, you talk to God?"

I said, "Yes."

"And you believe God talks back?"

"Yes."

All he said this time was, "Wow, that is really cool!"

God truly works in mysterious ways!

Shifting Our Perceptions

I don't talk or think much about the traditional definition of sin because I prefer to keep my focus on the other side of the coin, which is all about healing. So let's see if we can shift our perception about the word sin. The definition that works best for me is: Sin is "loveless perception." In other words, anything I do that does not come from a place of love could be called sin. Remember what Jesus said was the most important commandment? Learn to Love. This definition allows and encourages us to have a positive outlook in life. We don't have to beat ourselves bloody just because we sometimes lack the ability to love and to act from love. We are simply reminded to go again to the place of God and heal whatever is *blocking* our ability to love. This definition has worked really well in my life because it has shown me where my unhealed places are and it has given me hope that I can heal. I have been able to act in a more loving way in the world.

This definition of sin helps us recognize that there are many things we do because we don't feel loved or because we don't feel able to love ourselves and others. It demonstrates how important it is to learn to love ourselves first. When I love myself and know that I am made of God at my core — and I know that you are made of the very same Divine Spark at your core — it's easier to love and much harder to hurt.

We often think of sin as something we do that hurts another person, but let's go a little bit outside of the box and look at an example when sin, as loveless perception, involved hurting myself. I have struggled at times in my life with smoking cigarettes. (I know – gasp!) No, it is not written in the Bible, "Thou shall not smoke cigarettes," so in traditional terms I have not literally committed a sin. However, this behavior can be viewed as a very unloving thing I have done to myself. Through the lens of "loveless perception" smoking could be considered a sin. If I'm willing to hurt myself, I'm not being very loving, am I? The definition of loveless perception helps to uncover the places where I'm stuck and why — by not loving myself enough — I might choose to hurt myself. Lucky for me, God is in my corner and wants to help me heal this "sin" and love myself more. It's easy for me to take this to God and ask for help, instead of beating myself up for making this really bad choice. One of the verses in the Bible that helped me understand this issue, and others, in terms of loving my body was:

> What? know ye not that your body is the temple of the Holy Ghost which is in you?[31]

---

31   1 Corinthians 6:19

Shifting Our Perceptions

Sin and the Mind-Body Connection

A connection between our loveless perceptions and illness is clearly present. The Mind-Body Connection exposes the fact that repetitive negative and loveless perceptions toward ourselves and one another can make us physically ill. Jesus was well aware that we hurt ourselves when we choose to continue to repeat self-deprecating thoughts that result in sickness.

In the Gospel of John, Jesus healed a man who was sick. There is no evidence in this passage that the man had chosen to do anything hurtful or hateful to anyone else; he was just sick.

> Afterward Jesus found him in the temple, and said unto him, Behold, thou art made whole: sin no more, lest a worse thing come unto thee.[32]

In this example Jesus told the man to go and *"sin no more"* because he perceived the man's physical illness as the sin. Jesus knew that loveless perceptions were the result of believing we were unworthy and he understood the necessity of healing these unhealthy perceptions on physical, emotional, mental, and spiritual levels.

One day during a sermon at my Episcopal church, I was given another definition of sin that works really well, too. The priest said, "Sins are the obstacles we put between ourselves and God." By picking up our power and making a new choice, we are directed toward healing. Sin is anything that stems from our *belief* that we are separate

---

32   John 5:14

from God. We can never really *be* separate from God — even if we *think* so. And when we make a mistake, we are still not separate because God is always inside us, reminding us to return to healing through the application of more love. (We'll talk more about the problems created when we think we are separate from God when we discuss Adam and Eve.)

We All Fall Short

Sometimes the following biblical verse, which offers a negative definition of sin, is used as an indictment against us, further demonstrating our unworthiness:

For all have sinned, and come short of the glory of God.[33]

When we shift our perception, we see that this verse is nothing more than a statement on the human condition. As a person with a Soul housed in a physical body, each of us have temptations of the flesh — and we often find ourselves feeling unworthy of being loved. Then our ego takes hold and we do not thrive. Often we resort to acting out in survival mode. This verse simply tells us that it is part of our experience as humans to fall short. Life in the physical state (when we are "wearing" physical bodies) is more difficult than when we are in the glory of God (not "wearing" bodies), which is our "natural" state. Thus, we return to the dual nature of the human experience and we are

---

33   Romans 3:23

reminded that we are Divine and we are human. And again we are reminded of what is said in scripture: *What? know ye not that your body is the temple of the Holy Ghost which is in you?*[34]

> ### *Believing We Are Separate <u>is</u> a Temptation of the Flesh*
>
> When we look at our bodies, our "edges" made of skin, it is easy to think we are separate from one another: I end here and you begin there and there is a space between us, right? It's easy to get stuck in this definition of who we are. Instead, we must remember that the body does not define us. The body is what we wear; the Soul is who we are. In this way, we are all connected. Getting comfortable with this concept may take some practice, but when we shift our perception in this way, the words of Jesus make sense on a whole new level.

---

34   1 Corinthians 6:19

The Dark Side

Until recently, I didn't believe in hell at all. Then during an extensive conversation with my friend Ted, I came to realize that it *does* make sense that God created a separate place to honor our free will, in the off-chance that someone might stand before the Creator and say, "Thanks, but no thanks, I'd rather not be with God." Personally, I don't believe that any of us would do that when we lay our bodies aside and stand in the presence of God, but I guess it's possible. Ted pointed out that it is consistent with the nature of God, who created the free will system in which we live, to allow us to make the final choice. So, perhaps hell is the place God created for those who choose not to be with Him in Eternity.

The devil is often an excuse to deny taking responsibility for the choices we make in life. Evil may very well be defined as what happens when our ego is in full control, running the whole show, and leading us to make counter-productive choices. Perhaps the devil, or evil, is nothing more than excessive ego and lack of Self Love to the point of no return.

Second Coming

Perhaps we never thought of the devil and evil in this way before because we grew up thinking of God as being outside of us. With God outside, it makes sense that the devil is outside as well. But when we accept Divinity at our core, a shift in consciousness occurs and we are compelled to look at the potential for evil within each one of us. This shift in awareness requires that we accept responsibility for our own choices instead of blaming someone or something outside us for the bad things we choose to do.

Picking Up Our Power

A student in one of my classes once asked me, "But how do we pick up our power?" to which I replied, "By taking responsibility in your life."

He persisted, "Yeah, yeah, I know all that, but how do I get my power?"

I repeated, "By taking responsibility."

There is no magic pill here. The one who accepts responsibility for something is the one with the power to change it. When we blame someone else for things we don't like in our lives, we give them power over our lives. The opposite is also true: when we think someone else can make our lives better or happier, we give them power over our lives. When we are willing and able to accept responsibility, we automatically have the power to affect change in our own lives.

The Bible says we are to help and guide and love in order for our lives to be bright. It clearly states that we are not to be a stumbling block for others:

The Dark Side

> And if thou draw out thy soul to the hungry,
> and satisfy the afflicted soul; then shall thy
> light rise in obscurity, and thy darkness
> be as the noon day.[35]

> Let us not therefore judge one another any more:
> but judge this rather, that no man put
> a stumbling block or an occasion
> to fall in his brother's way.[36]

This verse has always been important to me, because the negative and judgmental treatment I received from fundamentalist Christians in my early life presented a stumbling block in my relationship with God. Those Christians hindered my efforts to find God and for a long time I felt as though they had actually taken God away from me. But I found comfort in the words of Jesus when he assures us of God's promise that no human can separate us from God:

> And I give unto them eternal life;
> and they shall never perish,
> neither shall any man pluck them out of my hand.
> My Father, which gave them me, is greater than all;
> and no man is able to pluck them
> out of my Father's hand.[37]

God promised us that, even if we are judged by others as being "not good enough," we still belong to God.

35	Isaiah 58:10
36	Romans 14:13
37	John 10:28-29

Second Coming

<u>The Way</u>

Always moving,
and not always forward,
It dances,
Ever changing
and always constant
Flow ...
    Ebb ...
        Tide ...

Lift ...
    Rush ...
        Hold ...
            Bubble and clap ...

I Am standing on the Bridge
with all of this
moving beneath me,
around me.
Holding me up
and letting me fall
as need be.

I cannot walk on water
and still it lifts me up,
Sustains me.

The Dark Side

I cannot walk on water,
but I know The One who can.
He is my Teacher
and he loves me deeply,
into my depths.
Where all color fades to gray.
Where all life sometimes
drains away
Leaving me lifeless ...
                Hopeless ...
                          Cold ...

There He holds me.
When no one else will,
or can,
He holds me
and loves even my darkness.

Living Water.

By Lily Phelps, April 9, 2011 (My Second Lent)

I AM The Way, The Truth and The Life

I have said for years, "I'm not a Christian *and* I follow Jesus." For many of my Christian friends this statement makes no sense at all because they do not differentiate between the two. For me, there is a difference and it has everything to do with the difference between what Jesus taught and the doctrine that came later.

Jesus came to this earth fully aware of his Divinity (God-Self) to teach us how to find God inside ourselves and how to live from that place. As one of my priests once told me, "God became man, so man might become Divine."[38] George Weigel, in the book *The Truth of Catholicism,* wrote, "The Son of God became man so that we might become God."

Christianity is a religion that offers an interpretation of the life and teachings of Jesus. I embrace most of it but not all of it. My spirituality is not about accepting someone else's interpretation. It is, first and foremost, about showing up fully in my relationship with God. One way I do this is by studying the life and teachings of Jesus. My greatest

---

38   Athanasius (b. ca. 296-298 – d. 2 May 373) Renowned Christian theologian, Church Father, chief defender of Trinitarianism and noted Egyptian leader of the fourth century.

issue is with the doctrine of some Christians who say that everyone *must* be a Christian in the same way that *they* define Christian. I don't believe this was what Jesus intended. Not believing all of Christian doctrine doesn't take away any of the passion and conviction I feel in my relationship with God. And in a very real way, it is not my business how God shows up in someone else's life.

What I can joyfully say is, "For me, Christ is the way." I believe Christ, the living energy of God, can show up in people's lives in ways we cannot possibly predict or understand, ways we cannot fathom. None of us knows how God brings together (re-members) the one body of humankind, what is called the Body of Christ, or how we are all made into *"one fold,"* as we read in Scripture below. I only know that *"With God all things are possible."*[39] It is not only none of my business how God makes this happen for everyone else, it would be arrogant of me to presume to decide what God can or cannot do. My business is to make sure I'm living the best life I can live, trusting in my relationship with the Divine and showing up passionately. Jesus said:

> Other sheep I have, which are not of this fold:
> them also I must bring, and they shall hear my voice;
> and there shall be one fold, and one shepherd.[40]

> And if any man hear my words, and believe not,
> I judge him not; for I came not to judge the world,
> but to save the world.[41]

Jesus is saying that he came to show *everyone* the way and that God will bring all of us into

---

39	Mark 10:27
40	John 10:16
41	John 12:47

I Am the Way, The Truth and The Life

"*one fold*" in the end. This does not mean that the followers of only one sect or religion belong to God. And it doesn't mean some followers are chosen as gatekeepers to hold others accountable for living life the way *they* (the humans) say it must be done. God is in charge of this. We must trust that God has ways of making things happen that we cannot possibly understand.

When Jesus said, "*I came not to judge the world, but to save the world,*"[42] he was telling us that God is more interested in what we're experiencing and learning in this earthly incarnation — and much more interested in gathering us together into one fold — than he is in the human details of how it all happens. Jesus makes a clear distinction between judging the world and saving the world. When we judge others as wrong, simply because their relationship with God looks different than ours, we are assuming the role of God and are not being a productive part of the plan to save the world. We must remember that God repeatedly tells us in the Bible that we are not to go around putting God's name on the stuff we make up:

> This people honour me from their lips, but their heart is far from me. Howbeit in vain do they worship me, teaching for doctrines the commandments of men.[43]

And again:

> Wherefore the Lord said, Forasmuch as this people draw near me with their mouth, and with their lips do honour me, but have removed their heart far from me, and their fear toward me is taught by the precept of men.[44]

---

[42] John 12:47
[43] Mark 7:6-7 (also Matthew 15:8-9)
[44] Isaiah 29:13

We are instructed to remember that the way each of us comes into relationship with the Divine is between each individual and God. These verses are examples of God reminding us that we need to be very careful because if we have to ignore so much of what God says in order to prove others wrong, we may be missing the whole point.

Detachment is the Ability to Not Be Offended

Learning healthy detachment is an important step in healing our inner conflict. When we are more attached to the outside world (the stuff in our physical lives) than we are to our inner Spirit, we develop expectations about how others should act. Then we get offended when people don't act the way we expect.

When I get really frustrated in my healing process, I look up to God and say (or scream), "What?!?" The answer that comes back is almost always, "Detachment, Lily. DETACHMENT!"

* This definition of "detachment" comes from Synergy Alliance, circa 1994.

> Jesus saith unto him, I am the way, the truth and the life: no man cometh unto the Father, but by me.[45]

For many people this verse is Jesus speaking *as* God, saying, "God is the way." The more fundamentalist Christian view is that the *only* way to God is to be a Christian, according to *their* definitions and traditions. I know many Christians

---

45   John 14:6

who disagree with this fundamentalist view.

"No one comes to the Father except by me." This is a statement about The Christ. It is not a challenge and it is not a criterion. It is a proclamation of Truth. Perhaps this does not mean that "I'm a Christian and you must be a Christian too, or you will burn in hell." Perhaps this is a "what is" statement — defining The Christ. Jesus never intended to divide us into warring factions, willing to kill one another to prove that we are chosen and they are not. Instead, this statement is a beautiful promise. Jesus is saying that he came to show us the way, and by living the way of Christ as he taught us to live, we *will* find the way.

> Jesus saith unto him, I am the way, the truth and the life: no man cometh unto the Father, but by me.

If you believe Jesus is God, then this statement actually says, "No one comes to God except by God." It's not a condition of membership or acceptance. It's a description of The Way. Our attachment to our humanness and our ego has convinced us that we are separate from God. We must be careful not to let this convince us that Jesus is separate from God, too. If you believe Jesus is God, there is no separation.

But we are human and our egos want to be right. We don't quite get it yet, so we continue to struggle, believing we are merely physical, all the while praying to be saved. We pray, asking God to "sanctify us" to "make us holy," but by constantly over-emphasizing our sin, we are, in effect, refusing to be sanctified. When we believe we are merely physical, a fallen people living in a fallen world, we are stuck. We find ourselves believing that Jesus came to save us *from* our lives, rather than to save us *in* our lives. We often forget that, with faith, there is really nothing to be saved *from* in the first place, because God knows the Divine Plan and God knows where we are headed. But as long as we hold tight to the belief that we are merely physical, we convince ourselves that we have not yet truly been saved.

Is this why some people believe *their way* is the only way? Perhaps they believe if they say the right words, they *will* be saved. Meanwhile, they continually remind themselves that they are sinners. Perhaps they have a hard time *feeling* saved. They reinforce an endless cycle of fear, not only by putting themselves down, but by judging others with their words, actions and definitions, hoping that someday they will be good enough for God. However, when the same system that teaches us to pray for sanctification says we are unworthy of actually being sanctified, we have a problem. If we are sinners — and it is arrogance, the very devil himself, to see ourselves any other way — then we never allow ourselves to be saved.

This is what happens when we only focus on our physical lives. But Jesus said:

> Labour not for the meat which perishes,
> but for that meat which endures unto everlasting life,
> which the Son of man shall give unto you:
> for him hath God the Father sealed.[46]

This verse illustrates one of the metaphors that has confused so many people. Being so attached to their physical existence, they often took his

---
46   John 6:27

I Am the Way, The Truth and The Life

words literally, not understanding that Jesus was speaking of the Higher Self, the Soul, which is eternal. This confusion continued later in this Bible story when Jesus said that those who eat his flesh and drink his blood will have eternal life. (John 6:53-57) Some of his followers left the movement at that point, because they thought Jesus was literally speaking of cannibalism. Jesus is calling us to remember that the *"meat which perishes"* is our physical existence (our human bodies and lives) and the *"meat which endures"* in eternity is our Spirit, our spiritual existence.

The instant we begin to relax our grip on our attachment to the physical and identify more with the Spirit of which we are made, we begin to vibrate at a higher frequency — and that's when we truly begin to be saved. Jesus speaks to us of The Christ and says this is the new way we need to learn to live.

Jesus said the most important thing we need to do is learn to love. Love takes time, and love comes in many forms. Jesus spent his whole human life being an example, showing us what real love can do and showing us the way. As we have discussed: He was a living, breathing human being who was completely aware of his Divine Spirit, as it exists in the physical human experience. He came to show, in very real terms, how to walk with a balance between Divinity and humanity. He left us with an assignment: that we learn to do this ourselves. "Follow me" doesn't necessarily mean, "worship me." It means, "You are just like me. Be like me."

"Do it the way I Am." Jesus said this is the way, the truth and the life. Live from this place.

God is ...

I often wonder why we try to define God, the indefinable. When we seek to make Divinity so easy to understand, we make God smaller and smaller. But what we're talking about here is God the Almighty, also known as the Great Mystery. By definition, God would not *be* God if we could easily understand all of Creation and the Divine Plan.

God Gathers All the Children

There is a lot of talk in religious circles about who gets into Heaven and who doesn't. I don't spend time thinking about this, because I believe we all end up together with God in the end. Some call this belief Universalism; I call it going Home or "re-membering" the Body of Christ. I don't know how this universal gathering happens, but I trust that God loves us all and is able to bring us all home together.

A representation of the idea that God ultimately gathers all of us together came to me in an unusual

Second Coming

way through the Bible story about Jesus feeding 5,000 men, plus women and children, with only five loaves of bread and two fish. As the story goes, after all the people were well fed, Jesus told the disciples to gather up all the leftover bread, and they filled twelve baskets with the leftovers:

> When they were filled, he said unto his disciples,
> Gather up the fragments that remain,
> that nothing be lost.[47]

The miracle is how Jesus and his disciples were able to feed all those people with so little food and having twelve baskets of leftover pieces of bread certainly adds to the mystery. But what called to me, over and over for many years, was the symbolism of bothering to gather up the fragments. Certainly, if Jesus could feed thousands of people at a moment's notice, with almost no actual food, he didn't *need* the leftover bread. So why did he do that? One day, as we explored this passage in my Bible Study group, I realized the answer, and I started to cry as I said, *"He who would not waste a crust of bread, would not waste me!"* Somehow, God gathers up all the fragments and brings us all home, because he values each and every one of us — equally.

Jesus didn't say only certain people could come to him. As a matter of fact, he went out of his way to extend himself to people nobody else wanted to be around, such as lepers, tax collectors and adulterers. He even empowered women in a way that was unheard of at that time. Jesus assures us that God "gave us" to him — and God will allow nothing to be lost:

---

47   John 6:12

> And this is the Father's will which hath sent me,
> that of all which he hath given me I should lose nothing,
> but should raise it up again at the last day.[48]

> In the last day, that great day of the feast,
> Jesus stood and cried, saying,
> If any man thirst, let him come
> unto me, and drink.[49]

In the following verses, Jesus speaks of God's timing, telling us that God chooses to call each one of us individually and in his own time:

> No man can come to me, except the Father which
> hath sent me draw him: and I will raise
> him up at the last day.[50]

> And he said, Therefore said I unto you, that
> no man can come unto me, except it were
> given unto him of my Father.[51]

We certainly have seen plenty of evidence that God loves us right where we are — and that God will find us at just the right time and in precisely the right way. All we need to do is trust that God knows how to get us home.

Jesus Was Radical

Depending upon your perspective, some of these ideas may seem radical, but when you think about it, isn't that how Jesus must have appeared in his

---

48	John 6:39
49	John 7:37
50	John 6:44
51	John 6:65

day? The word "heretic" is defined as: *one who holds controversial opinions, especially one who publicly dissents from the officially accepted dogma.* That is exactly what Jesus did. He gave voice to a way of living that conflicted greatly with established religious beliefs. He shook up the establishment every chance he got, and *the authorities did not like it one bit.*

Jesus was radical, and he spent his life bending the rules to show us a new way to live. But what if he hadn't done that? What if Jesus backed down when he was told to stop spreading his new ideas? He had to be smart and he had to be brave and strong. His love of God, his belief in the power of love in our human lives and his passion for us gave him the strength to go on.

Throughout the Bible we are given countless examples of religious leaders of the time trying to trick Jesus into saying the wrong thing so they could discredit him. Jesus knew the law, and he probably could have been a great rabbi with a long, happy life — one that wouldn't have ended in his being tortured, humiliated and crucified. The leaders were willing to let Jesus speak, until he started saying things they didn't even understand, things they certainly did not want the people to hear. The leaders knew the law and this had helped keep them in power over the people. So who was this guy who showed up, armed with all the training and knowledge he needed to be subversive — even revolutionary? And what did Jesus mean when he said, "Yeah, yeah, you've got all the details, but what about the Spirit of the law? What about love?" His stance was not subtle or insignificant then — and it is not inconsequential now.

God Is ...

The book of Isaiah, believed by many Christians to hold prophesy about the coming of the Messiah, talks about the coming of this new way when it says, "Behold, I will do a new thing."[52] In that same way, God is compelling me to write these words to you now. Christ is asking us to open ourselves even more and look to God once more in a new way. We do this not by throwing out the old way, but by expanding to a higher level of passionate relationship with God. That is radical.

Jesus shares a story about what he thinks of those who experience Christ in a different way. He tells his disciples not to forbid a man from doing a ritual (casting out devils) in the name of Christ, just because the man is not an official follower of Jesus. Jesus makes it clear that we, humans, are not to decide who is doing it right:

> Whosoever shall receive one of such children in my name, receives me: and whosoever shall receive me, receives not me, but him that sent me. And John answered him, saying, Master, we saw one casting out devils in thy name, and he follows not us: and we forbad him, because he follows not us. But Jesus said, Forbid him not: for there is no man which shall do a miracle in my name, that can lightly speak evil of me. For he that is not against us is on our part. For whosoever shall give you a cup of water to drink in my name, because ye belong to Christ, verily I say unto you, he shall not lose his reward.[53]

---

52   Isaiah 43:19
53   Mark 9:37-41

Radical Love Can Save Us

Once, when I had reached the end of my patience after being judged harshly by another, I said to God, "How do I do this, Lord? How can I not judge her as she judges me? How can I remember that she's a part of me and we are all a part of You?" God said, simply, "Keep looking forward." I understood this to mean that I should fill up with God's love, here in the present moment, and keep looking forward, instead of building up anger and resentment by looking back at all the times I felt judged. God was calling me to him and away from the things that were upsetting me. God was reminding me to forgive, let it go and move forward. This is another example of what it means to shift our perceptions and pick up our power:

> And when ye stand praying, forgive,
> if ye have ought against any:
> that your Father also which is in heaven
> may forgive you your trespasses.
> But if ye do not forgive,
> neither will your Father which is
> in heaven forgive your trespasses.[54]

When I'm Afraid

Sometimes I'm afraid of how other people may react to my way of experiencing God. In those moments, I take great comfort from Jesus and the way he stood strong and declared a new message, even though the establishment did not accept it.

---

54   Mark 11:25-26

God Is ...

He said we are to speak what God calls us to say to the world:

> But when they deliver you up,
> take no thought how or what ye shall speak:
> for it shall be given you in that same hour
> what ye shall speak.
> For it is not ye that speak,
> but the Spirit of your Father which speaks in you.[55]

I call this verse, "I'll tell you when you get there" and I take this statement to heart. This verse reminds us that God is always with us, even when we feel as if we have been *"delivered up."* We need not worry about what to say, if only we will listen to the Voice of God, also known as the Holy Spirit. Yes, sometimes I'm afraid. But I go where I feel myself being led and I do my best to go joyfully. Knowing that God is always with me helps greatly! For me, this is all about Faith!

Trusting that Spirit always leads me was important when I started going to the Episcopal church. During the entire first year I was there, I wondered, "What in the world am I doing in this Christian church?" Yes, I even questioned, "God, are you sure about this? Seriously?" But I knew God led me to that house of worship and those people for a reason, so I kept moving forward. The difficulty of that experience was compounded because some of my friends at my Spiritual Community felt that I had abandoned them. I told them, clearly and with compassion, that I did not choose to leave them. I simply did what I have always done: I went where I felt called to go.

---

55   Matthew 10:19-20

Second Coming

In my prayers I always say: "Show me where you would have me go, what you would have me to do and what you want me to say when I get there — and I will go joyfully." In all honesty, sometimes when I'm afraid I add, "And God, I'm struggling right now, so please don't stop nudging me forward, so I can go on, assured that you are with me." This is what I call "giving me the Cosmic Nudge." And on particularly tough days, I also add to the prayer: "Please push hard!"

> Lo, I am with you always, even unto the end of the world. Amen.[56]

To Love the Way God Loves

If we're all striving to live in right relationship with our Higher Power and we know that God is all about love, why do we have so many problems? Why is there so much fear? We're afraid to change and we're afraid to stay the same. We've been taught that who we are is not good enough, so we feel like we need to change something, anything. But change is hard and the old patterns hold tight.

In the following story, Jesus tells us that we need to pick up our power and truly own it so the seeds of good in our lives can take root and grow and we can produce good fruits. This verse makes it clear that we must be rooted in the Divine. We must let go of the dominance of the human ego, our doubts and fears, and our attachment to the riches of this physical life and be strong in God. How we do this is determined by our choices. We have to pick up our power and own it or the seeds will blow away and we will remain conflicted, unhealthy and offended:

---

56   Matthew 28:20b

God Is ...

> Hear ye therefore the parable of the sower.
> When any one hears the word of the kingdom,
> and understands it not, then cometh
> the wicked one, and catches away that which
> was sown in his heart.
> This is he which received seed by the way side.
>
> But he that received the seed into stony places,
> the same is he that hears the word,
> and anon with joy receives it;
> Yet hath he not root in himself,
> but dureth [endures] for a while:
> for when tribulation or persecution arises
> because of the word,
> by and by he is offended.
>
> He also that received seed among the thorns is
> he that hears the word; and the care of this world,
> and the deceitfulness of riches, choke the word,
> and he becomes unfruitful.
>
> But he that received seed into the good ground
> is he that hears the word,
> and understands it;
> which also bears fruit, and brings forth,
> some an hundredfold, some sixty, some thirty.[57]

Sometimes we *receive seed by the way side* when we simply do not understand what we hear or when we are, for some reason, not in a place where we can receive the gifts we are given.

Other times, we *receive seed into stony places* or *among the thorns* when we understand and are able to receive what is given, but we are not yet *rooted in ourselves* — not yet healed — so we cannot sustain what we have learned. Why? For some, tribulation

---

57   Matthew 13:18-23

might be said to come in the form of "sin" or from the devil; for others, it might be called ego and fear. Many things in this human experience can take away the peace of God. It is also inevitable that we slip into darkness sometimes, so Jesus reminds us that we must truly accept our own power and be rooted in the Divine within ourselves.

To receive God's seeds into good ground, we must prepare by doing our inner healing, so the seeds can take root and bring forth much fruit in our lives. In this scripture verse, Jesus emphasizes that we must have the root *inside* ourselves, not just outside ourselves, perhaps attached to doctrine alone.

Ego, Fear and Getting Un-stuck

When I look at life choices, I see most everything in terms of lessons that bring gifts. As long as I'm open to receiving, there is always a gift. Likewise, "wrong" choices are opportunities for growth and healing. Even when we make a mistake, nothing is wasted, because *"God uses all things for good."*[58]

> That which I do I allow not:
> for what I would, that do I not;
> but what I hate, that do I.[59]

This verse sometimes has been used as an illustration to remind us how bad we are, and how we always do the wrong thing even though we know better — demonstrating our sinful and undeserving nature. I'd like to take it in another direction and use it to help us look at the choices we make simply because we are human.

At some point in our lives, we've all said, "Why do I do things I know I do not want to do? Why can't I do better?" As an example, I offer an entry from my personal journal from many years ago,

---
58 Romans 8:28
59 Romans 7:15

when I first started to write this book. Notice how I vacillate between inspiring myself to overcome my own personal struggles and putting words on the page that might, someday, inspire others:

I'm starting this new deal today wherein I set aside a minimum of one hour every single day in which to write. In every writing class you take, they tell you to set aside the time — schedule it in. The idea is that you don't wait until brilliance strikes; you go after it, making room for it every day. I've done this before, but I can never keep it up. It has never become one of those "good habits" we all wish were easy to form. (Why is that? Why are the bad habits so easy to pick up and struggle with for a lifetime and the good habits — the rich, life-enhancing patterns and activities — are so dang hard to keep?)

And so, today, I begin again. I guess I need to focus on the fact that I'm actually doing it, I'm actually writing, rather than reminding myself of how hard it will be to keep doing this day after day. Then my mind turns to the question of why it's so hard to do that which I want so desperately to do: write this book! So many reasons spring to mind and, of course, that's exactly why I'm writing this book. I'm writing so that people can discover for themselves why they don't do what they dream of doing, just like I've had trouble doing in my life. What is it that holds us down? I'm writing this book as my own inspiration, and hopefully it will inspire others. It's that "And so on... and so on..." kind of a thing. God willing, the same things that got my butt up and off the couch will show other people the way, as well.

I will say to them, "Now keep in mind that your way is probably not the same, in detail, as my

Ego, Fear and Getting Un-Stuck

way. You'll see this illustrated many times as you discover that my way is not even the same for me from day to day. And my way has not always been the same at different times in my life. The ways change. The dreams may change. But the dreaming, itself, never changes. We all have dreams and, at one time or another, we are all afraid to reach for them. That is what this book is about: knowing you are worthy and able to reach for your dreams. That is the point."

And so it begins. This current inspiration to overcome my fear, and its attendant laziness, came from outside myself — from a friend who made negative comments about my parenting skills. These comments triggered me to go inside and look for growth opportunities. I guess we've got to take inspiration when it shows up, because you never know when the wind will fall out of the sails and you'll be left deflated, sitting on the couch, wondering where that inspirational gust went.

Now we're back to why we don't keep going when we start to do what we know we want to do. There are many reasons, not the least of which is that we have a lot of old habits, and we've trained ourselves over time to be very loyal to them. That's why these gusts of inspiration are so very important and why we must not miss a big whoosh! when it shows up. A big rush of enthusiasm inspires us to overcome old habits like sitting on the couch watching some stupid, mindless television show or getting on the computer to play an hour or two of a mind-numbing game or eating chocolate while reading the current copy of Rag Magazine cover to cover. Or how about spending money we don't even have on the Computer Shopping Store or sleeping too much every day. These are common examples of how we "numb out" in our daily lives, not to mention over-eating and the use of alcohol and other drugs.

Keep in mind, though, that we also have habits that are not so obviously counter-productive. The mind plays funny tricks on us when it's afraid to take a step into growth and healing. This is how our ego can take charge and convince us that "this" (insert your own destructive habit) is more important than healing our lives and learning Self Love. Some of us will clean our houses until they sparkle rather than take a class that could help us meet new friends or change our lives for the better. Some of us work for too many hours and convince ourselves that "work is a good and productive thing and nobody can criticize me for taking such good care of my family by working more hours than I get paid at a job that doesn't fulfill me and doesn't enhance my life or the world...." Oops, I just caught myself in the truth there, didn't I? We all make choices that don't serve us sometimes.

Even the things we do that are right and fruitful can become counter-productive when we take them too far. I am currently struggling with the fact that, as a parent, I have gone way too far in caring for my children. I coddle them and call it love. I do things for them that I should have taught them to do for themselves years ago — things they are perfectly capable of doing for themselves — things they actually do for themselves very well, when I let go and give them the chance to shine on their own. The really tough part of this lesson for me is that I want to believe they need me when, in fact, I need them to need me — and that's the real reason I do many of the things I do. And my kids aren't the only ones I take too much care of.

Ego, Fear and Getting Un-Stuck

You know this. You've been there, or somewhere like it. And you know this is not an easy thing to admit. I've been raising kids for so long that there is a part of me that's afraid to let it stop. A part of me doesn't know who I am if some child or man doesn't need me a thousand times a day. A part of me wants to hold onto the very things I've complained about all these years. And that's the mind twist: I've complained about everyone needing me and how I never have time for myself and yet, I am perpetuating the very things I've claimed to hate.

I'm reminded of a piece of scripture: "There is nothing from without a man, that entering into him can defile him: but the things which come out of him, those are they that defile the man."[60] And again I'm called to look at my own choices and take responsibility. Getting to this moment of realization now begs the question, "When did my kids stop needing me as much as I needed them to need me?" Have I spent years complaining about something they let go of a long time ago? If so, why didn't they tell me? Or did they, and I just couldn't hear them? "Mom, don't call him Baby anymore." (He was 13 years old.) "Mom, you don't have to cut my apples anymore. I'm a senior now." Or my husband saying, "Honey, the entire week you were out of town he got himself up and off to school without a word from me." I swear to you, these things and more have been said to me, word for word, by members of my family. And I bet you have your own examples of being stuck in counter-productive patterns. We perpetuate our own prison in so many ways, simply because it's scary to break free. It's an inside job — and our minds and our old habits keep us stuck until we figure out a way to set ourselves free.

---

60   Mark 7:15

Second Coming

A big part of our emancipation, the lion's share, does not pertain to people and things outside of us. It's inside us. "... But the things which come out of him, those are they that defile the man." We are stuck because we allow ourselves to be stuck. "...What I hate, that do I." Because being stuck in our old habits is as comfortable as old shoes, and moving on to new horizons is just plain scary. I'm comfortable with my lifelong habit of being overweight and complaining that there's nothing I can do about it. I won't have to fail if I never try. It may be true that I can't fail if I won't try, but I also will never succeed.

Striving for Balance

My Dad has always been a workaholic, a habit that is accepted in our culture, and it certainly was a better habit than my Mom's drinking. But he was gone all the time, and that wasn't a great deal for his kids. Yes, Dad was "bringing home the bacon," but for us, we felt abandoned, left with whatever scant resources my very depressed Mom could produce. Too much of a good thing is not always such a good thing.

Getting out there in life and taking a chance is invaluable. I protected my children to the point that I was wearing myself out. I was not helping them grow up and take responsibility for themselves. I was actually disempowering all of us at the same time — and it's not easy to disempower that many people all at the same time. One baby step at a time, I'm learning to turn these patterns around. I'm using the same amount of energy, focused in a new direction, to empower myself and others.

The Ability to Change

We have to try. We have to work hard and take chances, fall down and figure out how to get back up again. As adults, we have to do the same thing we're teaching our children to do: learn to fly! Take a risk, leap out of the nest and soar. But taking risks is not easy, and fear is a strong seducer — and an opportunity for ego to take charge. I'm reminded of something Jesus said:

> Repent for the kingdom of heaven is at hand.[61]

This is another verse that is often used to remind people that they are sinners and that they'd better hurry up and change or they're going end up in the fiery pit. But when we look at the word "repent" in terms of day-to-day, real-life experiences — and take the self-flagellation out of the words — "repent" actually means: *To change one's mind regarding past conduct.*[62] Here's the positive and uplifting interpretation I have written in my Bible: "Repent: A change of mind that bears fruit in a changed life." We can change our old patterns and make our lives new. We can stop doing what we hate to do. We can heal inside so the things that come out of us do not continue to defile us.

---

61 Matthew 4:17
62 American Heritage Dictionary

Second Coming

Healing Inner Conflict

After many years of applying my healing practice to outside conflicts, such as problems with other people, I took a leap in my evolution when I was able to take the process inwardly to heal my battle with food. I will never forget the day when I realized it was not the food's fault that I was fat! I was responsible for deciding what I put in my mouth. Sounds simple, but it's not. By not taking responsibility for myself, I blamed the food! When I learned to take responsibility, I picked up my power and was able to make positive changes in this area of my life.

Our Human Ego

Let's look closer at ego and how it produces fear. In my spiritual journey I have come to understand that the ego's purpose is to be the interpreter of the physical plane. The ego was created to help the Soul know how to live in a body, in a world of three dimensions and five senses. It interprets our experiences and helps us make choices. It was never meant to be in charge of our lives! When the ego demands to be in charge — and then lives in constant fear of its own obliteration — problems develop. Ego is in a constant struggle for control.

Some people say our spiritual work is about obliterating the ego. I don't think the ego can be destroyed, and we don't really want to eliminate it, since it is meant to be an important tool for us. The key is learning to keep the ego in its proper place, as the interpreter. We can learn to do this as we practice keeping God at the center of our lives:

> Jesus said to God, "Not my will, but thy will."[63]

---

63 Luke 22:42b

One of my friends once asked me about the meaning of this verse: "Are we supposed to sit around all day doing nothing but thinking about God and contemplating the Divine Plan?" Not necessarily, but we can choose to put the Divine at the center of our lives so we are in tune with the highest good as we move about our daily lives. This isn't easy, since ego keeps vying for control, but it can be done with awareness and practice. One of my favorite sayings from my spiritual journey and the 12-step programs is, "E.G.O. stands for Easing God Out." When we align with ego, we are pushing God out of our lives.

Keep in mind that when Jesus said, *"Not my will, but thy will,"* he was soon to be arrested, then tortured and crucified. He was under some serious stress! So in the moment, he was talking to God about his very human fear. He prayed to God, *"If thou be willing, remove this cup from me."*[64] In other words, "Papa, isn't there some other way we could do this?" Then he immediately said, *"Not my will, but thy will,"* and with that he surrendered to the will of God, whatever that would be.

Interestingly, before and after he said that, Jesus reminded the disciples not to *"fall into temptation."* This very well could be interpreted as, "Don't let yourselves go into ego and fear. We must stay aligned to God's Will." How is this any different for us? It's not. When we are afraid, we are susceptible to the will of the ego and the fears that come with it. Remember, there are two aspects of our lives here on earth: we are Divine and we are human. We are an eternal Soul contained within a temporary, physical body. Ego is part of our

---

64   Luke 22:42a

physical existence, and when ego is in charge it is very tempting to focus our thoughts, our hearts and our lives on its attendant fear and survival techniques. Jesus knew all about this.

Yes, Jesus was probably afraid, because he was human. But Jesus knew he was also Divine, so he acknowledged his human fear and then let it go. He surrendered to the Eternal aspect of His being, that which gives life a deeper meaning. He surrendered to God in all forms. Then he was free!

Sneaky Ego

Our culture tells us that ego is synonymous with egotistical — being self-absorbed, thinking we are better than other people. But ego is sneaky, and it doesn't always show up that way. Because ego is constantly in fear of losing control, it will do whatever it takes to keep us from following Spirit, even if that means cutting us off at the knees. Take my ego, for example. It often tells me that I'm *not as good* as other people. This may sound like humility, but it is actually fear, and it often causes me to do the wrong thing in an attempt to make myself feel like I'm good enough. As a result, my ego pushes me to work harder, do more, and be better so other people will like me. While my extra effort seems like a positive way forward, ultimately it is counterproductive to do "good stuff" from a place of fear.

What is productive about fear and pain is that they definitely get our attention. When we are aware, we can make better choices in terms of how to respond to the fear and pain. Our culture teaches us to deny, deny, deny. We shove icky feelings down and pretend they are not there. But when we hide from our feelings, that's all we are doing. The feelings are not really gone and unfortunately, they often rise up and reveal themselves in awful ways. We project our fear and pain onto others. We tell people what they should or should not do or feel or value. Meanwhile, we are denying our own feelings about what is going on inside ourselves. After all, we have convinced ourselves that nothing is wrong with us, so it must be about the other person, right? This realization is very important as we learn how to respond to the ego.

We might be tempted to think our emotions are the problem. We all have emotions and we acknowledge them or we don't, but the problems occur when our ego attaches itself to our emotions. For example, perhaps we are sad and we decide that the reason we're sad is because someone else did something. Ego is very good at deciding who to blame for our feelings, our problems and our difficult lives. When ego decides whose fault it is that I'm angry or hurt or when I don't have what I want, that is a misalignment. When ego is in alignment with Spirit, it doesn't blame, it simply describes. And when ego is aligned with Divine Will, it provides information and fuel for life and healing. A misaligned ego will keep us hooked into what other people think of us — and it can suck us dry in a heartbeat. Ego, as interpreter, can help us find a clear path to the healing power of God.

When Fear Is In The Driver's Seat

Once when I was in a new relationship with a man, things began moving too quickly and we both got scared. This is an excerpt from an e-mail I sent to him:

"My very wise daughter [Katie] helped me put a lot of things in perspective today. One of the things she had me look at is the way I overreacted when I went so deeply into fear about your safety. She reminded me that this is not how I usually am. She pointed out that the woman I was acting like was an example of what fear can do to people, and she was quick to remind me that the "woman in fear" is part of who I am and it cannot be denied. One of the most profound things she said was, "Fear turns us into different people... either temporarily or forever ... depending on how much we let it control us." So I'm thinking that this is where you and I find ourselves today, and now we have a choice: We can stay in fear and push each other away ... Or we can face our fear and push through it, either together or separately. Katie also said, "The way people deal with their fear is one of the most important things you can know about them and often you don't find this out about someone until way further down the road." This gave me hope! Yes, we got caught up and we moved too fast and freaked ourselves out, but we also learned some really valuable things about ourselves and each other. And now we get to decide what to do next. I would like to think it is possible to work through this together."

It is not easy to allow such vulnerability in "real life," but facing our fears is at the heart of healing our lives. When we can work through conflicts together, it builds and strengthens our relationships and creates greater intimacy. This kind of deep inner work can feel like you are willingly walking into the fire, but this is the only way to heal our inner wounds so we don't have to continue to act out our pain.

Ego and Depression

I suffer from depression. I've struggled with this wacky form of brain chemistry since I was a teenager, so a big focus of my spiritual practice has been on healing this affliction in my life. If you have never experienced the debilitating effects of depression, it may be difficult for you to truly understand how it feels. How can I describe what it is like to wake up every morning wishing you were dead, even though you are quite aware that you are very blessed in your life? There is no logic to it, and there are no words to make it go away. Having spent many years on my spiritual healing practice, I'm grateful to say I have been depression free for most of the past six years — the longest period of time in my adult life. So this is a very big deal. I still have bad days, like we all do, but nothing compared to what it was like to wake up every day for years inside a dark, painful cloud of debilitating despair that came from nowhere and left me powerless to control it.

I went through a pretty tough stretch late in 2011. This time, the depression was different than it had been before, because its cause was situational, rather than chemical. I was laid off from my job. Many of you have experienced this: You work hard all of your life and you do your job well; then, without any warning an economic downturn appears at your doorstep. The company you work for starts to fail and expenses have to be cut somewhere. This experience brought up all my deepest fears, including my old friend, Miss I'm-not-good-enough.

Toward the end of this four-month period of depression, dark thoughts began rising up from inside of me and I spent too much time beating myself up about all the mistakes I have made in my life. I'm talking about deep, dark, self-hatred, with thoughts like, "If people really knew me, they wouldn't love me." I even said to myself out loud, "Why did God pick me to write this book? Why didn't he pick someone better, someone smarter, someone who doesn't make so many mistakes? People will find out that I'm human and I've screwed up in my life and they will use that as a reason to decide that what I say about God loving us is false. I will let God down!" I wallowed in the muck like a champion one night, writing it all down as quickly as I could so I could really get to the heart of it and heal it.

Finally, God's light came into my heart and I wrote down this statement, "All I have to do is remember that I am good enough for God, just as I am." And then what I believe was the voice of God came to me in comfort: "Stop trying not to hate yourself and love yourself like I love you. It's a lot nicer this way." It was so interesting that God said, "Stop trying not to hate yourself" before reminding me to love myself. I certainly was deep into fear and darkness, and I became aware that I was trying to

Ego and Depression

> **Deep Dark Work**
>
> A realization came to me one day that I wish I had known earlier in my life. When we are in the darkness of depression, we think we're not doing anything productive and feel like we are worth absolutely nothing as human beings. In reality, we are working so hard on the inside that we have no resources left to do much of anything else.

hate myself at a very core level. It's just so hard to feel worthy sometimes.

One night while talking to one of my Christian friends, he shared his personal version of "I'm not good enough." He said something like, "I just think that no matter how much I do, there is always more I could do for God." I told him that I understood how he felt, but with a small shift in perception, perhaps he could see it a bit differently.

"Of course," I said, "there's always more good we can do, but it seems to me that you're keeping score. You're so focused on not being able to do enough, which translates into keeping track of more and more things you think you *should* be doing. It's almost like you're trying to earn enough points to get into Heaven. The problem with that thinking is, if we're not careful, we have a tendency to start keeping track of what *other people* do too, as a way of convincing ourselves that we're good enough."

Our personal feelings of lack are projected onto others, because we're afraid of what we are feeling inside about ourselves. If we're not careful, we start telling other people they aren't doing enough, or they aren't doing something right. Before we know it, we've taken the focus off of ourselves — how to do things better in our own lives — by shifting our attention to someone else. We end up proclaiming how someone else should change to make our own lives feel better. This never works, but that doesn't stop us from doing it.

At this point in the conversation with my friend, I felt myself shift into what I call a "Bliss Moment." Whenever this happens, my voice becomes full of passion, I start looking starry-eyed and it's as though I feel myself being lifted up. I said to him, "What I do is slightly different." I described how my healing, and the nature of my relationship with God, help me shift into states of Divine bliss and I can feel God's love embrace me — and that makes me *want* to do better. There's no keeping score and no need to feel unworthy. I just feel bliss! And I want to stay in this presence forever and share it with everyone.

Getting there is only a shift in perception, but this bliss is certainly not how most of us were raised. It's not always an easy transition, but we can learn to live motivated by love, instead of fear. It takes a lot of baby steps and patience and prayer, but it does happen in the fullness of time.

As someone who has suffered from the effects of depression for decades, it is an absolute blessing to experience a relationship with God that lifts me up from such a place of darkness. Did you notice what happened when my friend came to me struggling with feelings of unworthiness? I was able to rise above the same fear that caused me to suffer in my life and become a light for someone else. This is just one example of the beauty that happens when we glow with God in the world. Being in service to others lifts us up as well!

Developing a Spiritual Practice: What Do I Do?

What are some of the things you might do each day to develop your Spiritual Practice? Here's a list of some of the things I do as a matter of course:
- I listen. I put this first on the list, because it is critical for innumerable reasons.
- I practice a spiritually based method of conflict resolution. This is the foundation of my Spiritual Practice. I have learned to view conflict as a valuable learning tool, rather than something to be avoided in life.
- I pray, and not just the formal "Dear God" kind of prayer. For me, prayer is something I consider doing in any given moment. For example, when I see people on the street holding signs asking for food or money, I "zap" them with a beam of love. I send them a little prayer, and in the process I am showering the love of God out into the world.
- I go to Bible Study every Tuesday morning at 6:30 a.m. (Yeah, ya gotta want it bad to get up that early, but it's really that good!)
- I remind myself to "Let go and let God." This is a big challenge for me, because I'm a recovering control freak. Surrendering to the will of God is not something I thought I would ever be able to do. For most of my life, it wasn't even something I wanted to do! But I finally learned that surrender is not about giving up control as much as it's about shifting the focus of control. When I finally surrendered to my own Soul, God within, to the Holy Spirit as it moves in and through my life, everything in my life shifted toward Peace. When I remember this, and live by it, my life works better than when I forget and let my ego and my human mind take control again. It can be a constant struggle, but I have learned to be in this flow more consistently over time. That's why it's called a Practice.

... more later ...

Second Coming

Light in the Darkness

When I read the Bible, I look for how it relates to my life, right now. When I studied the Book of Zephaniah, it spoke to me of the desolation that depression brings to the afflicted, the effort of the ego as it struggles to maintain control, and the ultimate saving Grace of God. This story begins by describing the terrible things God says can happen when we don't listen to the Divine Voice. It echoes our discussion about ego domination, with its attendant fear-based thinking, and what happens when we are out of balance and not aligned with the Will of God.

Zephaniah describes the days of wrath, which accurately reflect the darkness one experiences in the depths of depression:

> That day is a day of wrath, a day of trouble and
> distress, a day of wasteness and desolation,
> a day of darkness and gloominess,
> a day of clouds and thick darkness . . .
> When we shall walk like blind men . . .
> Neither their silver nor their gold
> shall be able to deliver them.[65]

The story then reveals the freedom and joy that is felt when we are no longer held in captivity by ego and are in accord with the Will of God:

> Seek ye the Lord, all ye meek of the earth . . .
> The Lord their God shall visit them, and turn away their
> captivity . . . This is the rejoicing city that dwelt
> carelessly, that said in her heart I am,
> and there is none beside me.[66]

---

65   Zephaniah 1:15-18
66   Zephaniah 2:3, 7 & 15

Ego and Depression

The third chapter of the Book of Zephaniah drives home the point that without care, one can return to the darkness, just as we all do sometimes. It makes a final reference to the sneaky ego that tries to prevent Spirit from saving us, by rising early and getting to us first:

> Woe to her that is filthy and polluted ... She obeyed not the voice; she received not correction; she trusted not in the Lord; she drew not near to God ... The just Lord is in the midst thereof; he will not do iniquity (wickedness): every morning doth he bring his judgment to light, he faileth not; but the unjust knows no shame ... Thou will receive instruction ... But they rose early, and corrupted their doings.[67]

Hope and healing are introduced at the end of this chapter: Aligned with the Soul, with Spirit, we are able to heal. These verses speak of relief from the pain. They speak of forgiveness — by the Self (capital "S" signifying our Soul) and by God — for the mistakes we have made and the promise of God to remove *out of our midst* (from inside of us) the suffering caused by pride and haughtiness of ego. It further assures us that our Spirit is mighty and that we will be saved from the pain of ego and will be aligned with Spirit again:

> For then will I turn to the people a pure language
> that they may call upon the name of the Lord,
> to serve him with one consent.
> In that day shalt thou not be ashamed for all thy doings,
> wherein thou hast transgressed against me:
> for then I will take away out of the midst of thee

---

67   Zephaniah 3:1-2, 5 & 7

Second Coming

> them that rejoice in thy pride,
> and thou shalt no more be haughty.
> The Lord hath taken away thy judgments,
> he hath cast out thine enemy ...
> The Lord is in the midst of thee;
> thou shalt not see evil any more.
> The Lord thy God in the midst of thee is mighty;
> he will save, he will rejoice over thee with joy.
> I turn back your captivity before your eyes,
> saith the Lord.[68]

Perhaps you are wondering if I believe the Book of Zephaniah was written to show people how to heal from depression. No, I don't. However, if a story written around the year 625 BC about the struggles of a group of people can bring me inspiration now in the 21st century, what difference does it make if that is why the story was written? The things we experience in our outer reality are a reflection of what is happening inside of us. Yes, I understand that in this particular Bible passage the people were being warned and called to change their ways. We *are* the people.

---

68   Zephaniah 3:9. 11, 15, 17 & 20

Out There and In Here

Often when we read stories in the Bible, our first interpretation leads us to separate people into two categories: some are viewed as good people and some are judged as bad. The story of Zephaniah focuses on a group of people, some of whom were in trouble. No one can argue that, from a literal reading of scripture, but by only looking at this story literally we can limit the scope and impact of the text.

Once we step away from seeing the story as being about only "those people," we realize these passages are about people everywhere. Strict literal interpretations may be problematic in several ways. They may cause us to apply the lessons only to specific groups of individuals and they may lead us to judge people only in terms of "us" vs. "them." Once we take it upon ourselves to start deciding who is good versus who is bad, an opportunity may arise for the ego to assure us that "we are good" and, therefore, anyone who disagrees with us is bad.

A dramatic shift happens when we read a story and assume it may be talking about each one of us, in the here and now. This is an important discernment to make and it's an important tool you can use in your own life. Going back into the story, it says, "The Lord is in the midst of thee." Taken literally, this means the Lord is in the midst of this group of people. Now, let's apply it to ourselves, with an inside perspective and allow the power of the lessons in the story to teach us something very valuable about ourselves. We find:

Outside Perspective	Inside Perspective
The people are in darkness	I'm depressed or struggling in my life and in fear of my own darkness
God brings joy to the people	Loving God and following the voice of the Holy Spirit brings me to the Light
The people fall back to their evil ways	Depression and darkness return and/or I stumble on my Path for some reason
God, ever patient, speaks even more clearly, causing the people to thrive by casting out the enemy and bringing joy	God finds me wherever I am and, speaking even more clearly, shows me how to shift my focus from my enemy (ego, fear, depression) to my Spirit (The Christ) so I can heal and live in joy

Out There and In Here

Developing A Spiritual Practice: What Do I Do?

- I practice Self Love constantly, and I do everything I can to inspire others to love themselves.
- I meditate, which sometimes is the same as prayer for me. People who meditate regularly might say I'm doing it wrong if I'm thinking words when I meditate. I get that, but after all these years, sometimes I still have trouble clearing my mind, so I catch myself praying in bits and pieces when I meditate. I also practice moving meditation, while walking, since I don't sit still well. And I love to go to that quiet inner place while I wash dishes or fold laundry.
- I practice mindfulness, which is about paying attention to what shows up in front of me in my daily life.
- I set my intention. This means that I make a conscious intention to find what I'm looking for. Then I remember to take action on what I find.
- I look for signs from God everywhere in my life. This inspires me to go inside and cultivate my inner relationship and go outside with love in my relationships with others.
- I go to church.
- I read constantly. I choose the Bible, of course, but I also read everything I can about how to heal my life and be closer to God. Since God comes through each one of us in a different way, I love to read other people's stories about their Spiritual Journey. And one of my favorite genres is Science Fiction. It is amazing that Science Fiction can be so deeply spiritual.
- I write and journal. This helps me get clear on what I really feel and what I want to feel once I let the peace of God into my being. I even send myself text messages as reminders.

... more later ...

Second Coming

Inside

I know a place
Where dreams are coming true
Right now ... As we speak ...
In real time

It can take a while to get there
A Journey that is, as all good Journeys are,
Deep and rich ... Dark and mysterious

Always worthwhile in the end,
But try telling that to the tourists who throw trash on the lawn
And actually come for a good time created by someone else

This place is not like that.
You have to show up, full-force and naked
Standing in your own honesty
Glowing and raw and sure of it

The one requirement is
That you suspend all belief in fear ...
lies and lack ...
And road maps

You won't need any of those things anyway,
But some are so hard to convince
That we no longer even try

There is an orange cat here
Who never sheds
And music is played at your slightest request

Out There and In Here

The wizard who lives here is so gifted
That you will actually learn
About this very moment in your present life

It can be slippery, these layers of naked truth
Doing our best not to hide or morph
Into what we see outside.

The tiny twinkling lights remind us
Not to fall out of the tree-house
And back into "real life"

by Lily Phelps, January 31, 2009

Second Coming

About This Poem, and Writing or Journaling In General

Writing is a powerful tool on my Healing Journey. It is critical, as I process the details of my life in order to heal, because it forces me to get really clear about what I'm feeling. Sometimes I write letters to people, as I process my own inner conflict. Often I don't even send the letters, because by the time I finish writing them, I have reconciled my inner conflict and I no longer need to speak to the person with whom I was upset.

Writing is also important because it leaves a paper trail that shows me how far I have come. I try to remember to put dates on everything I write so that, years later, when I find a piece I've written, I have "historical context," telling me where I was then versus where I am now. This gives me hope as I move into the future.

In 2009 when I wrote the poem "Inside" I was dating a man at the time and all the words in the poem related to how I felt about him. What's really cool is that I found this poem years later and realized it was also about me! During those years I had grown in Self Love and had reclaimed more of my power in my relationships with men, so I was able to see the "wizard" in me, as well.

Another example of writing that evolved with the writer took place when Teresa, Barbara and I were working on our first book, *Diaries of a Psychic Sorority*. Teresa and I had an experience in which we were certain that words had literally changed on the page. The difference between where we were in our healing when we originally wrote the piece, and where we were when we were editing it only a few months later, was staggering! We refer to this earlier time as having been in a "deflated sense of self." And now we can laugh about it!

What's It Really Like? Real-Life Doubts and Fears

The following is a journal entry from 2012. I have come a long way in terms of keeping ego from controlling my life, but this shows a fairly current example of how my sneaky ego almost got the best of me:

I had "words" with Teresa on the phone this morning, which triggered my old pattern of feeling like I'm "doing it wrong." But this time I immediately began processing my own inner conflict. In the past, I've been too focused on the outside, letting other people's opinions matter more than my own opinion of myself. But I'm learning. This new experience was awesome. (I say this with little enthusiasm, because I'm still crying, but I want to get this down on paper while I'm feeling it.)

First, I let Teresa know, right in the moment, clearly and kindly, that I didn't want to talk anymore. I didn't stay on the phone, pretending to be OK until I could get off "the nice way." Getting off the nice way always involved pretending nothing was wrong, which was a lie, but in the past I often was too afraid to do it any other way. This time I didn't stay on the phone and process with her. Instead, I hung up to process my own feelings, fears and inner conflict.

The things Teresa said were true, but I sensed a funny tone in her voice, and I took it personally, even though she might have been upset about something else...or nothing else, for all I knew. I chose to let myself feel like I was doing it wrong again! When she called, I had been reading the transcript of a conversation I had with a fundamentalist Christian

Second Coming

Minister years ago, and experiencing that again already had me a bit off center. It makes perfect sense that Teresa's comments about the man I'm dating left me feeling a bit shaky and triggered feelings of insecurity. I simply need to remember that I'm not doing it wrong just because someone disagrees with me. And I need to remember that ego waits for these moments of emotion and fear to pounce.

So, where is my ego in this? Oh! That's easy: the Minister with whom I had the conversation kept telling me over and over that he wasn't judging me, and that told me that he was totally judging me. Then he finished our meeting by saying he would pray for me! Re-reading that conversation had already shifted me into fight-or-flight mode. And the new boyfriend: How dare he not like me as much as I like him?! When I put these two emotional topics together with Teresa's comments, which were difficult for her to say and difficult for me to hear, my ego voice started screaming things like, "That's not right! Why aren't they listening to me? Don't they know how great I am?" Oh, my sneaky ego — always wanting to be right — when what I really need is to be at peace and listen to myself and to God. I simply need to remember that I'm worthy and I'm good enough without having other people tell me so.

So, what does all this mean in terms of healing? It means my emotional attachment to outside "stuff" is much more balanced than it used to be... and my ego is still looking for a weak spot. It means I have to remember to stay connected to Source and not let ego take hold of me. It means we don't get to stop being human! We are here to learn these things ... Learn to Love ... starting with Self.

Out There and In Here

You've heard people say, "Get a life!" Well, I don't need to get a life, because I already have a really great life. The only thing is, I ignore my great life a lot! No wonder it drives me crazy when people don't respond to me the way I want them to and I feel ignored. The inner conflict comes from the fact that "I ignore me all the time!" I put my life on hold while I wait for someone or something (often a man!) to come and make it better for me. Over and over, I find myself back at Self Love 101.

No wonder God reminds me constantly to go back to the most basic lessons. The cycle continues until we get it right, so it's best to go back to what we know and try it again in a better, more healed way. Amen.

A Note About Speaking the Truth

> "And ye shall know the truth, and the truth shall make you free."[1]

In the journal entry you just read, we see an example of how our tone of voice often reflects our nervousness about things we need to say to people. Teresa was doing her best to speak with Compassion as she shared a difficult, but necessary, truth with me. Of course she was nervous; she loves me. But we learned long ago how important it is to speak the truth, always with Compassion, even when it is difficult. Our culture doesn't teach us this, so Teresa and I are really grateful that we have each other. It's a precious gift to have people in your life whom you can count on to always tell you the truth. Yes, sometimes that truth is difficult to hear,

---

[1] John 8:32

Second Coming

but the alternative is wondering when your friends are lying to you simply because they don't want to hurt your feelings.

Keeping Tabs on the Ego

So what happens to ego when we are healing and experiencing great progress on our spiritual journey? When you have been healing for some time and you've started to feel a certain degree of success, a release from fear is experienced — and it feels really good. Aspects of your life that you thought you'd never master begin to come into alignment, and you have so many aha! moments that you begin to believe the clouds were created just so you could walk in greater comfort. It's an amazing feeling to be this high, especially when you think back to where you came from and where your life was just a few short [fill in the blank: weeks/months/years/decades] ago. Anyone can apply this realization process and feeling of peace at any stage of life. The truth is that if you stay focused and keep healing, you will continue to be amazed throughout your lifetime of practice.

What good news it is to be on this kind of a roll. You are looking at your own internal issues, you have been diligently tending your own emotional and spiritual garden, and you have been reaping the spiritual rewards that come from this level of introspection and healing. You are truly beginning to experience synergy: the regeneration that comes through human will and Divine Grace. At some point, you may feel inspired to share this amazing process and your exciting experiences with those around you. And why wouldn't you want to share what has, quite literally, saved your life? And so you turn to those around you and ...

Stop!

This is an important moment and one that most of us come to many times during our healing journey. This is the moment when you get to decide *if* you will share and *how* you will share your spiritual experiences with others. Depending upon what you decide, this is the moment when you could either be a light in the darkness of someone else's life or you will become the know-it-all who thinks she's the only one God has been talking to all this time.

So stop and be very mindful of the fact that your ego has been waiting for this very moment. While you've been busy healing and praying, your ego has been very busy becoming resentful of the fact that it is no longer in charge of your life. Your ego has had weeks/months/years to prepare for the moment when you think you know something that someone else simply must hear about. Be careful, for your ego is going to make its move now.

Trust me on this. Your ego is raging — and it's been waiting for the chance to get even. It's not infuriated at the people who *you* think need your wisdom in order to straighten out their lives. No, your ego is mad at you — and it's going to try to

Keeping Tabs on the Ego

cut *you* off at the knees so it can move into the palace and have its control back before you even figure out how to stand back up again. I've been there, more than once.

What are your options? I can't tell you what you *should* do, because that's the whole point: *you* have to figure out what to do. I can, however, tell you what you *will* do, probably more than once along this journey: You'll decide that you've got your ego in check and you'll go out and try to help other people. Don't get me wrong, helping other people is a beautiful thing. It is right and good that we share our stories and our light with others. *And you will probably underestimate your ego more than once in this process of learning*

This is not a bad thing; this is an inevitable thing. You will learn so many lessons from this part of your journey, and all the bruises you get along the way will be well worth the experience. Just know that whenever we turn to another person and say, "Let me tell you something ..." we run the risk of believing that we have something they don't, that we are special, that we are God's chosen and were sent here to save someone other than ourselves. It's human nature. It's part of the process. When you turn to share your wisdom with someone else, *you* might learn much more than the other person from the experience.

The truth is, I hope you *do* learn something from these moments, because that is why you are here: to learn from experience. If you come back talking about nothing other than what somebody else learned from you, then you missed the point. Instead of helping someone else, you might have been feeding your ego — and in the process you failed to receive the gifts that are part of *your* healing process. What a shame, since *you* are the one you came here to heal.

If you remember nothing else, remember these words:

> The goal of this mission is not the healing of the planet.
> The goal of this mission is the healing of the self.
> The by-product is the healing of the planet.[69]

This is a direct quote from the Divine. Do not minimize it. Do not forget it. My job is to heal me and your job is to heal you. Period. Everything else is icing on the cake and not our primary focus.

I know that sounds strange. Why shouldn't we help other people? We should. But we have to do our own work first, and very thoroughly. Otherwise, we might think we are helping others when we're actually only massaging our own egos. There is a very fine line between helping and fixing, between sharing and pontificating — and when we cross it, our desire to help others becomes more about *our* lesson in ego management than it is about *their* lesson in Self Love. Take time to read this chapter again. (And if you're angry that I keep mentioning the ego, pay attention to your red flag because your ego may already be running amuck. If so, you might want to read it yet again.)

This is what happens on the spiritual path: We keep thinking we're here to do something else or heal somebody else, but we can't. We just end up wasting a lot of time and energy pretending we can. (Note: I shouldn't really say "waste," because God uses all things for good, so nothing is really wasted. It's just that our energy is not being utilized

---
69   Synergy Alliance

effectively.) Once we learn our way through these moments of ego, we can see more clearly where to place our focus.

Faith When We're Afraid

Sometimes spiritual people assume they are not supposed to have doubts and fears, because when we are in faith, we feel supported and guided from on high. We simply trust God. But we are still human and we *do* have doubts and fears — and it wouldn't be honest to pretend otherwise. So when we are scared or really sad, what do we do?

I struggle because I know that the lives of so many others are so much more difficult than mine. I wasn't abused as a child. I'm not living with a life-threatening illness. I have never been hungry or wondered how I would feed my children. So what do I have to be afraid of? The way I see it, whatever they are, our fears are real to each one of us. It is important not to say, "It could be worse so I shouldn't feel this way," thereby minimizing our feelings, instead of healing our fears. We feel what we feel — and the sooner we acknowledge it, own it, and take responsibility for what is ours, the sooner we can release the fear and return to balance. This is when faith plays a pivotal role in our lives.

> Now faith is the substance of things hoped for, the evidence of things not seen.[70]

Faith envelops us and helps us believe even when we're frightened. Prayer, and an ongoing spiritual

---

70   Hebrews 11:1

practice, are important, because these tools give us a strong foundation for the difficult times when we don't or can't believe much of anything in the moment. By building my foundation, or my spiritual practice, when things are going well in my life I cultivate faith — belief that does not rest on logical proof or evidence — so I'm stronger when the going gets tough.

It's important not to wait until we are struggling or terrified to begin building our spiritual foundation. I heard it said this way in a prayer at my Episcopal church, using the symbolism of the Communion table: "Deliver us from the presumption of coming to this table for solace only, and not for strength; for pardon only, and not for renewal." The priest spoke about the sacrament of Communion, a ritual that affirms our living relationship with God. She talked about the bread and the wine, which represent the life force of Christ. She said bread and wine are simple food that then becomes something greater when we realize they bind us together in Spirit and empower us to follow the same path that Jesus walked. And are we not like that bread? Are we not simple humans who become something more when enlivened by the Spirit?

Keeping Tabs on the Ego

Memo From God:

"The Gift is Never Given in Only One Direction."

Giving and receiving creates a complete circle, a flow, one that we often interrupt as human beings. I used to have trouble receiving from others. "Oh, she is such a giving person" may sound lovely, but I was stopping the flow and it created problems in my life. God once said to me, "If you continue to refuse to receive, your ability to serve will begin to diminish." I got the message, and I have been learning to receive ever since that moment!

When I counsel people, and when I'm teaching or speaking in public, people often express their gratitude to me. I say, "Thank you," of course, and then I express my gratitude to them in return, reminding them that I'm equally grateful for what they have given to me. Often people are surprised when I thank them, because they think they are the only ones who received something from the experience.

Remember that the gift is never given in only one direction. Be aware of how this flow works in your life. As the old saying goes, "You get what you give." It's important that we learn to give that which we want to receive, because this circle of energy also flows in the opposite direction. When we direct negativity toward others, we create an energy flow that does not support our well-being. I like the saying, "If you want love, give it away!"

Developing a Spiritual Practice: What Do I Do?

- I talk to people all the time! I'm lucky in this area, because I'm comfortable talking with people who don't usually talk about God or Jesus or the Bible. My background outside of religion helps a lot with this, because I don't see myself as different from anyone else. I don't judge others as being wrong, so they don't feel judged when talking with me. People tell me, "I can't believe I'm having this conversation. Usually when people start talking about Jesus, I tune them out, because I expect to be judged harshly." It's sad to think of all the God Moments that are missed because of judgmental, fearful people.
- I take classes and workshops so I can learn new tools for my practice.
- I have Bliss Moments. This feeling that comes upon me, often out of the blue, allows me to feel God's Presence and it lifts me up. When I experience a Bliss Moment, I often call or text someone I love and say, "I'm having a Bliss Moment and I just wanted to share the feeling with you." People with whom I'm really close support me when I'm down, so I make sure they also get to fly with me when I'm at my highest.
- I remember that I am experiencing Divine Union when I make love with my partner. This is what sex is truly meant to be: a living expression of uniting with the Divine. Looking at it this way, it's seems sacrilegious to go out and "just have sex."
- I try to eat healthy food. I have to work hard on this, because my relationship with food has been challenging. I'm still learning that my body is to be cared for as a temple.
- I use affirmations and inspirational messages. I put them on paper and post them all around my house (and in my desk drawers and in my purse and as bookmarks) as reminders to be mindful, present and awake.

Keeping Tabs on the Ego

- I reach out. I send my friends (and myself) text messages that express bits of Divinity that come to me throughout the day.
- I schedule sessions with healing practitioners. I might choose to experience hands-on healing to help move energy through the body, or I might meet with my chiropractor/acupuncturist, Natalie, who totally rocks my world. I might take part in a drumming or chanting group, which is like meditation with a soundtrack. Or I might go to a retreat center, like Clare's Well, for a healing session or massage with one of the beautiful Franciscan nuns. Or perhaps I'll join a group that includes ritual. I have a lot of options here.
- I don't judge my insides by someone else's outsides. Some people look as if their lives are so perfect, but we must remember that everybody has inner junk they need to heal. Just because someone looks good on the outside doesn't mean they are all sunny on the inside. Remembering this helps me to cut myself some slack!
- I do yoga, and when I was younger and physically more able, I did karate. Yoga is an important part of my spiritual practice, because it puts me in touch with my body in a positive way. Religion sometimes makes our bodies out to be bad ... sins of the flesh and all that. That kind of thinking keeps us disconnected from the wisdom of the body, which is the temple of the Holy Spirit. Our bodies are the vehicles that transport our Spirit in this earthly life. It is important to honor the body. When we do that, we are much less likely to commit "sins of the flesh," so this is a good practice for those who think that way.
- I take Communion to honor my personal relationship with God and witness myself as a living member of the Body of Christ.
- I use music. I love to listen to secular music, even love songs, and pretend God is singing to us.
- I smile a lot!

... more later ...

Heaven On Earth

To Walk On Water

The following is one of the most important and life-giving stories in the Bible. Most of us have heard the story of Jesus walking on the water, but did you know that Jesus called Peter out of the boat to walk on the water with him? And Peter did step out of the boat and walk on the water:

> And in the fourth watch of the night Jesus went unto them, walking on the sea. And when the disciples saw him walking on the sea, they were troubled, saying, It is a spirit; and they cried out for fear. But straightway Jesus spoke unto them, saying, Be of good cheer; it is I; be not afraid. And Peter answered him and said, Lord, if it be thou, bid me come unto thee on the water. And Jesus said, Come. And when Peter had come down out of the ship, he walked on the water, to go to Jesus. But when Peter saw the wind boisterous, he was afraid; and beginning to sink, he cried, saying, Lord, save me. And immediately Jesus stretched forth his hand, and caught him, and said unto him, O thou of little faith, why did you doubt?[71]

---

71   Matthew 14:25-31

Can you believe that? Jesus simply says, *"Come,"* and Peter, a mere mortal just like the rest of us, got out of the boat and walked on the water just like Jesus did! Then he got scared, started to sink, and Jesus said, *"Oh, man of little Faith. Why did you doubt?"*

Don't we all do that sometimes? With faith we step forward, and then we doubt and fall back. This is exactly where I'm sitting right now, as I write this book: I got out of the boat and started to walk on the water. And very often I'm afraid. Then comes the revelation: All I need to do is have faith and keep walking next to Jesus. (As I write this I start to cry. It never ceases to amaze me how much reassurance I need sometimes.)

Another favorite idea of mine in scripture states clearly that, if we have faith and let go of our doubts, we can do just about anything. And how much faith do we need? We only need faith as big as a mustard seed, one of the smallest of seeds. For years, I have carried a tiny glass bottle full of mustard seeds in my purse. When the time is right, I give them to people. It's a cool reminder of what the Bible says:

> And the Lord said, If ye had faith as a grain of mustard seed, ye might say unto this sycamore tree, Be thou plucked up by the root, and be thou planted in the sea; and it should obey you.[72]

Jesus tells us again, in the Gospel of Mark, that with faith, we can remove our doubts so we can do what he did. He also reminds us to forgive others. That's an important part of the process of healing our own fear, because it is harder to stay in fear and judgment when you are in the act of forgiving:

---

[72] Luke 17:6

> Jesus answering saith unto them, Have faith in God. For verily I say unto you, That whosoever shall say unto this mountain, Be thou removed, and be thou cast into the sea; and shall not doubt in his heart, but shall believe that those things which he says shall come to pass; he shall have whatsoever he saith. Therefore I say unto you, What things soever ye desire, when ye pray, believe that ye receive them, and ye shall have them.
>
> And when ye stand praying, forgive, if ye have ought against any: that your Father also which is in heaven may forgive you your trespasses. But if ye do not forgive, neither will your Father which is in heaven forgive your trespasses.[73]

In this verse we see that, through faith, we can manifest what we desire in our lives. It is helpful to remember that the word "manifest" does not mean "to create"; it means "to reveal." Jesus references this when he says, *"What things soever ye desire, when ye pray, believe that ye receive them, and ye shall have them."* Everything we need for our highest good is already part of Creation. We just need to have faith that our highest good will come to us.

We also need to remember this: What we *need* and what we *think we want* is not always the same thing. In the words of a song, "Some of God's greatest gifts are unanswered prayers."[74] Life includes tough lessons that might be called "the gifts that don't come in pretty packages." Just as steel is forged and strengthened in a furnace, these experiences create who we are in the fires of life, making us stronger for the next challenge we will

---

73   Mark 11:22-26
74   "Unanswered Prayers" by Garth Brooks

encounter. Sometimes it is difficult to see the gifts we are given, especially when they are painful, but with faith and patience, we can find some of our greatest gifts in the most difficult of experiences. When Jesus called Peter out of the boat to walk on the water, he expected Peter to believe it could be done. Belief is essential to the process of removing our doubts. In order to receive, Self Love is also crucial — seeing ourselves as worthy of receiving something good so it will happen. And we must have faith.

---

*Manifestation and the Law of Attraction**

This is something Spiritual People talk about a lot. This universal law says we attract into our lives that which we need for our highest good. Sometimes it is what we want, but it is always what we need in order to learn, heal and grow. Life can be so tough at times, because we are learning the hard way.

Spiritual People often pray for "This or something better" to give the Great Mystery (God) room to move in and through their lives, for their highest good and the highest good of all.

One of the toughest lessons in my life taught me this: In the end, I didn't get anything I thought I wanted, and yet, I got absolutely everything I needed.

Our ability to know ourselves as worthy, Divine Beings is key to the Law of Attraction. Our capacity for Self Love affects our capacity for everything else we experience in life. It's not just about saying affirmations and telling the Universe that you want a million dollars. It's about doing deep, inner cleansing and healing to release the doubts and fears that keep us from believing we are worthy of having whatever is our highest good.

*The Law of Attraction came from the New Thought movement in the early 1900s

In the story, Jesus also speaks of the importance of being willing to forgive others. This clearly shows that forgiveness creates a circle: If I will not forgive myself, I'm not as likely to forgive others, and the reverse is also true. All of this — faith, belief, forgiveness, healing our doubts and fears — help us experience the kind of lives we hope to have for ourselves. The voice of God put it this way: *Passion to manifest the Divine Intention creates Heaven on Earth.*[75]

Forgiving Others – Judge Not Lest Ye Be Judged

Judge not, and ye shall not be judged: condemn not, and ye shall not be condemned: forgive, and ye shall be forgiven.[76]

And he saith unto him, Out of thine own mouth will I judge thee.[77]

Jesus reminds me that I will be judged as I judge others. If I judge others harshly, then I will be treated the same way in return. And when I remember to share love and compassion, I trust that this is what will come back to me. I don't know about you, but I would much rather be judged in love and compassion.

To avoid judging others harshly, it is important to look inwardly and take responsibility for ourselves and our own issues first:

---

75   Synergy Alliance
76   Luke 6:37
77   Luke 19:22

Second Coming

> And why beholdest thou the mote [speck] that is
> in thy brother's eye, but consider not the beam that
> is in thine own eye? Or how wilt thou say to thy
> brother, Let me pull out the mote out of thine
> eye; and, behold, a beam is in thine own eye?
> Thou hypocrite, first cast out the beam out of thine
> own eye; and then shalt thou see clearly to cast out
> the mote out of thy brother's eye.[78]

We heal when we ask forgiveness for our own shortcomings, the "beam in our own eye." And we forgive ourselves before we even think of offering to help remove the speck (mote) in the eye of our friend. During this process, it's important to remember the presence of the sneaky ego. Healing myself first helps to assure that I'm not speaking to someone else from an unhealed place inside of myself. By not *"offering to help remove the speck in the eye of another"* before tending to myself, I'm able to remember that it is not my job, or even my business, to go poking around in someone else's garden uninvited. If someone needs help removing their specks and nurturing new seeds in their garden, they will seek and find help. Be careful not to run around trying to fix everybody else, tending their gardens, while your own garden is being overrun with weeds.

Jesus tells us that he did not come to judge us, and he reminds us to keep our focus on a higher perspective:

> And if any man hear my words, and believe not,
> I judge him not: for I came not to judge the world,
> but to save the world.[79]

---

78   Matthew 7:3-5
79   John 12:47

> ### *"Judge Not Lest Ye Be Judged"*
>
> What helps me remember this idea is a funny quote from my days of healing with Synergy Alliance: "Choose your words very carefully, for someday you will have to eat them."

Remember, we will encounter problems when we believe everyone else has to agree with our way of thinking and doing. When we get really clear on what works for us, and stay aligned with Spirit, it is easier to stop judging the way other people behave. Obviously, I believe my way is right for me or I wouldn't do it this way. And your way is right for you. And yes, we can help one another find the way, but we are not meant to intimidate each other by stating that our way is the only way. We are to trust that God's Way is right — and God can find a way to reach each one of us. Another person's journey is none of our business.

> Let us not therefore judge one another any more: but judge this rather, that no man put a stumbling block or an occasion to fall in his brother's way.[80]

Too often we judge others harshly and act out hatefully when we are afraid that we are wrong, because our ego, doubts and fears are at play. When we trust that God will find a way to each one of us at just the right time, we can relax. This is when prayer and faith support my journey. I don't know how God finds everyone, but when I refrain from judging others as wrong, I can step back and let God be in charge.

---

80   Romans 14:13

> Therefore judge nothing before the time, until the Lord comes, who both will bring to light the hidden things of darkness, and will make manifest the counsels of the hearts: and then shall every man have praise of God.[81]

Remember, this is not just God saying that the darkness in everyone will be brought to the light. This is God talking about everything inside each one of us. When we take our struggles to God, and know that Divine Light is shining upon us and inside us, we can have faith that our darkness will be taken away.

At this point you may be thinking, "But I do forgive and hold others in compassion, and they aren't always forgiving and compassionate to me." This is often true in our daily lives, but holding others in compassion will lead you to be more compassionate toward yourself — and this can change your life dramatically, even when others don't reciprocate. We never know how much our compassion soothes the hearts of the people who need it most, simply because they may not know how to give it to themselves or to others. It's a process, and I assure you that your life will be enriched when you are able to be compassionate and forgiving.

Forgiving Ourselves First

This one was a huge breakthrough for me!

> If any man come to me, and hate not his father, and mother, and wife, and children, and brethren,

---

81   1 Corinthians 4:5

> and sisters, yea, and his own life also,
> he cannot be my disciple.
>
> And whosoever doth not bear his cross, and come
> after me, cannot be my disciple.[82]

Initially I was told that the first part of this verse meant we should hate and push away our own family if they weren't "Christian enough." I never understood how Jesus, who taught that love was the answer, would encourage hate of any kind, much less hatred of our family and even our own life. Then one day I was struck by a new truth. Read the verse again and consider this possibility: Jesus is not saying that we *should* hate our family and our life; he is saying that we *do!* He is also saying that he can show us how to heal so we can turn from hate to love!

Jesus is saying we must first acknowledge that we sometimes hate even the people we love the most. In order to heal, we need to take responsibility for the things we do that cause hatred to arise. We need to own it, bear our own cross, and then release it to the Divine. When we don't accept personal responsibility, we come to Christ pretending that we are already whole, and we say things like, "I don't hate my own life and I would never hate anyone!" Until we learn to accept our judgments, learn from them, forgive ourselves and others and let it go, we are not as prepared for discipleship as we think we are. In fact, we are inhibiting our own healing by the façade we wear — and Christ knows he can't move forward with us until we accept this and come before him in truth and humility.

---

82   Luke 14:26-27 (stated twice)

Second Coming

The Greatest Lies Are the Ones We Tell Ourselves

Many years ago, my Synergy Alliance friends experienced a spiritual curriculum we called "I'm a liar." We shifted our focus to the areas in our lives where we were rationalizing our own behaviors, due to fear and doubt. We all do this at some time or another. For example, when we date someone and a lot of red flags arise — but we like the person, or we are just plain lonely so we ignore the warning signs and justify staying in a relationship that we know is not right for us. Many of us also choose to ignore the signs that we are drinking, smoking, or working (insert your habit of choice here) too much and lie to ourselves until we ruin our lives.

When we lie to ourselves, we abdicate our own power and we miss opportunities to heal. Instead of taking responsibility, we do things like blaming the guy for hurting us, even though the red flags told us what was going to happen right from the start. When we are caught in our addictions, ego, and fear run amuck and we tend to blame other people and circumstances for the lousy state of our lives.

What's the point, really?

Kobayashi Maru

Star Trek television series. It was a test given to all candidates for the position of starship captain. The interesting twist was that there was no way to win in this test. None. Unless you were the heroic genius, Captain James Kirk, who figured out a way to cheat the test. The point of putting these candidates through a test they could not win was to see how they reacted under the extreme pressure of facing a no-win scenario. It may have been a good exercise for a starship captain, but the stress level bordered on psychologically damaging. What does Kobayashi Maru have to do with us? Do we really think God has given us a life that we cannot possibly win no matter how hard we try? I don't think so.

When kids today play their video/computer games, they have what is known as a "cheat code." It's a way to win when they can't find any other way to win. Using this analogy in our lives, the "cheat code" is to stop thinking of yourself as merely a physical being. The "cheat code" is to rise above the system: to acknowledge the Spirit inside your body and begin to identify with it. When we do this, we aren't actually rising above the system, because the system is no longer a part of the game; it is no longer important to "win," just as it was never meant to be important in the first place. Jesus talked about not getting so attached to the law and the physical details that it causes us to lose sight of the Spirit. Yes, the law is important, but the most important thing is to know that we are love! Everything else is just a detail.

We can rise above and view life from a new perspective so we don't feel like we're caught in a game we cannot possibly win. Jesus, the Messiah, came to fulfill the law — and he said that to fulfill the law we must learn to love. Then, everybody freaked out! The priests naturally wanted the law to be important, because it allowed them to remain in control and keep the power that it brought them. And the people wanted Jesus to make their lives easier so they would not have to do anything for themselves. So for a lot of people, what Jesus said was a real problem.

Jesus said that he is eternal, and so are we, and he demonstrated that only the body dies. He prophesied his own physical death and then died on the cross, betrayed and bloody, right in front of the eyes of his followers. And in three days he came back to life. "Ta-da! See, it's just as I told you. Here I Am." By this point, everyone was really freaked out.

Fast forward to the present. Yes, many of us believe Jesus is God, but then our fear causes us to separate ourselves from him, because we can't possibly be as exceptional as Jesus. But this is what Jesus told us *not* to do. He came and did exactly what he said he would do *and* he showed us, with plenty of examples throughout his life, how to live by focusing on the presence of God inside us. And how do we respond? Just like they did back in the day — we freak out. The question then comes to mind in a new way: If we believe Jesus died for us, then why won't we heal for him? Why not wake up and let him take us where we are going, sooner rather than later?

> **"Reality is Free.
> It's the Illusion You Have to Pay For."**
>
> This statement is one of the most profound things God has ever said directly to me. Reality, from the perspective of God, says that we are made of Spirit, and Spirit is eternal. The illusion is the belief that we are merely physical beings in a physical world. We all know that none of the stuff we buy will follow us into Eternity, and not a single physical thing endures forever. What endures are the lessons and gifts that come from our experiences. These are what shape our Souls and prompt our Spirits to evolve. These are taken into eternity.

Picking Up Our Power

I find it interesting and a little disheartening when I meet people who are very committed to their religious life but are also committed to the idea that we can't *do* anything to help save the world. Often these people have a bleak outlook about our collective future, and they seem to have resigned themselves to the belief that only God can save us. I certainly believe in the Power of God and I often think it will take a miracle to save us, but I don't think the Lord wants us to just sit back on the couch, numbed out by television or something worse and wait for the Apocalypse. Yes, we need God, but what about picking up our God-given talents, passion and power and taking some steps of our own? Personal piety is a beautiful thing. Humility is a beautiful thing. But when we take that too far, it can turn into, "I have no power and it's all going to end in doom anyway." Meanwhile, we suffer while our world is slowly beating itself to death.

A minister expressed to me many years ago that he doesn't think peace can happen until the Messiah comes again. He said anything short of that is a human effort — and it will fail. He said, "It's just not going to happen. We're too tribal, too tainted with sin."

What if God wants to be here now? What if The Christ awakening in each of us is the answer to all our problems?

This is how God responded to these questions many years ago in a message to the Synergy Alliance group:

> "You can have all the Divinity. You can have all the answers. You can have all the knowledge, right here at your fingertips, in all of the Universe.
> In fact, it is there for you.
>
> But if you do not choose to pick up your power, all that is for naught. All of that knowledge sits on the shelf and gathers dust while your world beats itself to death."
>
> "What will it take to get you to stand up?"

Let me share a little story, a dream, perhaps: There's a really big boat and a bunch of people are rowing in the boat, but they're scared and they're all panicky and everyone is rowing in a different direction. Over time, leaders emerge and they get everyone to listen and some start to row in the same direction. Then others start to calm down and they join in the rowing. Others are still afraid, so it's slow going, but a shift is starting to happen. Eventually the boat will arrive at its destination, the Divine Destination that the Creator has known about all along. It's the one Jesus came here to teach us about. We will get there, sooner or later.

Picking Up Our Power

It all depends upon how long most of us stay in a state of fear and panic. Now remember, it's a really big boat, and it has been navigating throughout the millennia, with billions of people cycling through billions of incarnations. But we *will* get there. God is very patient. Can you even imagine the kind of patience it takes to wait for us to learn to love ourselves the way God loves us?

In reality, it doesn't make any difference *when* we get there. Time only matters to us in this three-dimensional experience where we perceive time as being linear with a beginning and an end. But God doesn't experience time as we know it. God is outside of time. In the end, *what* we believe may not even matter, since we can't prove the Universal Truth from our vantage point here on Earth. Perhaps what is most crucial is that we all passionately believe in something life-giving, something higher than ourselves, so we can rise above all the fear and believe in ourselves as an expression of Spirit. God, being infinitely patient and, of course, already knowing how the story ends, isn't worried about our struggle here on Earth, because he has infinite confidence in the Divine Plan. Even all the billions of us, as afraid as we are, cannot disrupt the Divine Plan of the Creator.

That sneaky ego emerges again — how odd to think that we can screw up the Divine Plan! And what's truly out of balance is when we think we are powerful enough to have an impact on God's plan and simultaneously believe we are totally unworthy and cannot do anything right. No wonder we're scared!

And now we return to the debate about free will. What would be the point of God creating a free will system that doesn't acknowledge our self empowerment? Imagine God saying, "Now, my Beloved Children, you go and work really hard and make beautiful children of your own and toil and suffer and care a lot. But in the end you cannot make a bit of difference, because I have already set it up so you are doomed to fail. Oh, except maybe a few of you whom I will bring to Heaven with me, but the rest of you, no way." I simply cannot accept that.

God's Will and Our Call

In a workshop meditation at my Episcopal church, we were instructed to focus our gaze for several moments on a picture in front of us. Then we were guided to come back to our physical reality, keeping in mind the experience of the moments we spent with the image. The picture I looked at was a beautiful close-up of the face of Jesus as he was gazing off to the side. In that brief meditative moment, his gaze turned directly toward me and as a single tear came to his eye, he simply said, "You know." Startled by the power of his gaze, and through curtains of my own tears, I replied, "Yes, Lord, I know." In that moment, I was not conscious of anything else. It was as though I knew everything. In that moment, I felt God. I knew God.

Some would say that "picking up our power" somehow usurps the power of God, as though the only way God is strong is if we are weak. But what if, by refusing to pick up our power, we are actually denying God's Will for us?

What's It Really Like Healing Inner Conflict? To Really Pick Up Your Power?

Here is a scenario that can be really tough to swallow: Your partner (he or she) leaves you yet another aloof message about why he cannot be or do whatever it is that you want him to be or do. You fly into a rage about what a lousy jerk he really is and who does he think he is treating you like this after you've given him so much and gotten nothing in return and he can't keep doing this and "I swear to God I'm gonna ..." We all know the words and, unfortunately we all know the feelings and the heartbreak that go along with the words when you're in love with a man who is a ...

Now stop. Ask yourself some questions like:
- "Why am I still here letting him treat me this way?"
- "Why do I think he will treat me better than I treat myself when I'm sitting here letting him treat me like dirt?"
- "Why wouldn't he want to be with someone like me who gives so much and seems to be content getting so little in return?"

When you stop and turn the situation around, you begin to see what you are doing to perpetuate the problem. I spent much of my life being mad at men because they didn't treat me better than I treated myself! This is not about blame; this is about self-responsibility and personal power. This is about seeing where your power lies, picking it up, and moving on with the gift of the lesson tucked neatly under your arm. I promise that when you stop blaming other people for treating you the way you let yourself be treated, you will be hit smack in the face with your own power.

This is not to say that he's not a lousy jerk. Maybe he is, but if that is true, then why are you still there? This is what healing looks like from the inside out. Changing yourself. Changing your own life.

Letting Go of the Title "Sinner"

I know some Christians who seem to fight for the title "Sinner." They constantly repel the idea that God gave us everything we need to make this life work and that it's up to us to pick up our power to make healthy, loving, Christ-like choices. Some people ask God to forgive them, and they are forgiven, but they still refuse to forgive themselves and continue to judge themselves as sinners. So what is the point in God forgiving them in the first place? If we adopt their perspective — that the whole system is set up for us to fail and nobody can win — why even bother to try in life?

I suggest the opposite: Nobody can prove how the system is ultimately designed and we won't know how it works until after we're dead, so let's stop squabbling over details and simply let the Light in.

I have refused to call myself a Christian, not because I don't love, accept, and follow Jesus but because of the darkness and judgment that is often attached to the word "Christian." People who recite pre-scripted words and claim to be Christian, but are not Christ-like in the world, are not serving in the spirit of Jesus. I left the mainstream church in the first place because of such hypocrisy. This behavior flies in the face of everything Jesus taught us about living a good life.

Being Christ-like in this world is not only important, it is our birthright and our responsibility. Yes, God's Grace is present, but we need to show up and participate. That's why the Bible says, *"So faith by itself, if it has no works, is dead."*[83] Each and every one of us is a child of God, and Jesus came here to teach us how to be a child of God to the fullest extent possible.

Memo From God ...

How about you worry less about sin and love each other more? Let's try that!

And let me know how it goes, because I really do love you and I want you to be happy.

---

83   James 2:17, NRSV

Letting Go of the Title "Sinner"

Grace or Works – How About Both!

Years ago, when I was still really angry at Christianity, feeling that Christians had taken Jesus away from me, my daughter Katie helped me find some peace. She reminded me that sometimes the ideal, which is wonderful, does not match the execution. In other words, sometimes people cannot live the words they speak. Spiritual People call this "walking your talk" and it is challenging for all of us to walk our talk at times.

The ideal of being a Christian would be better served if people spent their energy striving to be Christ-like in the world. Some Christians, however, believe this is wrong, stating that the only way to salvation is through God's Grace. They say being Christ-like is not the way to God, because it could lead us to think that good works will get us into heaven. Perhaps this is so, especially if we allow our ego to be in charge, but Jesus taught us to live from Spirit, and being Christ-like in the world is all about living from Spirit.

Jesus speaks of the importance of the things we do (our works) in Matthew 16:27: *"For the Son of man shall come in the glory of his Father with his angels; and then he shall reward every man according to his works."*

In John 10:38, Jesus even calls our attention to his own works several times: *"... Though ye believe not me, believe the works: that ye may know, and believe, that the Father is in me, and I in him."*

While I certainly believe in and appreciate God's Grace, in my humble opinion, God would also like us to show up and be actively Christ-like in the world.

Beginning of The End

The process of writing this book has taken me to a whole new level in my spiritual development and maturity. One thing I have learned is to stop making excuses: I believe what I believe and I don't need someone else to tell me it's OK. I am strong and clear in my relationship with my Creator and that is the only approval I need. Coming to this place within myself has taken me a lifetime!

I once heard this definition of Right Work: "When your greatest passion meets the world's greatest need." I have asked God many times, "What is Right Work for me? What can I do to set myself on fire with passion and also meet a need in the world?" Early in my Spiritual walk, I received my calling. God told me that *"I am a teacher and a sower of seeds."* That became my life path. It sounded so simple at the time, but it has taken 21 years (so far) for me to embody those words. And I'm still being transformed through this experience on new levels every day.

So I am a seed planter. After receiving this information, it didn't take long for me to realize that the one who plants the seeds is seldom the one who waters the seeds and is almost never the one who harvests. My first reaction to this awareness was frustration, because I wanted to be there to see the harvest, the moments when people realize their gifts. But soon I began to accept myself as a seed planter — one who drops a tiny idea in a fertile spot and urges it on with a little nudge. My calling is simply to allow myself to be led and to share what I am given with others. What people do with these seeds, if anything, is between each individual and the Creator, and their choices are none of my business.

So I asked myself, "What will I teach and how do I want to teach it?" I immediately knew that I couldn't be the kind of teacher who says, "I'm the teacher, which means I get it, and you're the student, which means you don't." That's not how I'm made. So I set out to teach people that they don't need me. I'm not special, but I do have gifts to share, just as each of us do. The challenge is to find our gifts and then use them.

One of my gifts allows me to break complex ideas down into simpler pieces that help people understand more and inspire them to find their way. I discovered this ability while raising my children. The experience of parenting my three beautiful children and seeing them become productive, happy, healthy adults has been one of my most important life purposes.

It is essential for each of us, as human beings, to express ourselves passionately as we live our lives. I'm here to be me and learn what that means as completely as possible. I'm here to live my life and make my own choices. We are all learning how to choose our way back home — back to God — or not. Each of us certainly has the right to choose

The Beginning of The End

our way forward, wherever we want to go. In my life, I choose Jesus as my teacher, my example, and my friend.

Why were we created in the first place? What in the world are we doing here? The best answer for me is: We come into this life to learn about love on a whole new level — love of the self in relation to "the other." This can only be done when we perceive an "other," which is what our physical bodies and seemingly separate experiences are about.

Our eyes and other senses tell us that our physical bodies are separate from one another. I end here and you begin there, and the empty space between us represents our separateness. The journey to wholeness takes a giant leap forward when we realize that we are not separate from one another at the Soul level. That's what the term "Body of Christ" means to me; we are all part of one Divine body.

Free will enables us to choose our perceptions and behaviors. As humans we have the opportunity to choose love, or not, in each moment of our lives. What we experience is the natural consequence of whether we choose love — or not.

The struggle intensifies when we not only perceive ourselves as separate from one another, but also view ourselves as separate from God. When we experience God as something outside ourselves, just like other people, we may interpret God as our judge, rather than simply as our loving Creator. First and foremost, we must practice Self Love and acknowledge the indwelling God, which is *always* present in our lives. Our culture doesn't champion this perspective, which is why the example of Jesus is so important to me.

> **Learning By Example**
>
> God sent himself into the world in the person of Jesus with the awareness of the God-Self active and present. This offered us a living, breathing example of how to be the Image of God inside a human body.

Spiritual people use the concept of "mirroring," which is a metaphor for how we learn through our relationships with one another. A mirror allows us to see something that we cannot see on our own, such as the back of our heads. In every relationship, we have the opportunity to learn something about ourselves as a result of how others respond to us. Other people can show us things we can't see without their reflection — our blind spots, so to speak. We look into the "mirror" of the other person. Jesus understood the concept of mirroring. This is why relationships with other people are so valuable: they are tools for self-reflection and understanding.

We can choose not to engage with other people, but even if you lock yourself in a dark closet and don't come out, you're still learning what it's like to sit in a dark closet. You may refuse to be in a relationship with others and refuse to grow as a human being in this way, but you're still learning something about yourself sitting there in the dark. And unless you really love sitting stubbornly all alone, you're probably learning a lot about the "not love" side of life. It's pretty impossible to *not* learn anything and the simple act of learning *something* is an important part of what we're here to do as human beings.

The Beginning of The End

It is a beautiful thing when we are available to one another for all the teaching and learning that life offers us and to share life's experiences with one another. Even though we're not really here to heal anyone else, we are here to heal ourselves — *and* we are all doing it together. What a beautiful dance of great cooperation!

Genesis Revisited

> God speaks to each of us as he makes us,
> then walks with us silently out of the night ...
> You, sent beyond your recall,
> go to the limits of your longing. Embody me.[84]

As human beings, much of our struggle is the result of not grasping the fact that we are made of God, and *then* we have a body. As the great Christian writer C.S. Lewis said, "You do not have a soul, you are a soul. You have a body."[85] We are, first and foremost, Spirit, the very image of God. Now let's look closer at the place we started, in the Book of Genesis:

> And God said, Let us make man in our image, after our likeness.[86]

For a long time, I wondered, "Who is the *us* in this verse?" Then I realized: It is *us!* In the beginning, before we came into human form, we existed with God and as God. In the beginning, before we wore

---

84 Rainer Maria Rilke
85 C.S. Lewis, Mere Christianity
86 Genesis 1:26

these bodies and walked the Earth, there was only one of us: one God, one Spirit, one us. Then God (still us) decided to create human bodies to house our souls so we could have unique experiences that were not possible when there was "only one of us" and we were only Spirit. When there was only God, only one of us, we could not do certain things without the presence of an "other" to do them with us — and to show us who we are.

We took on physical bodies so we could experience the Self in relationship to the other. Experiencing ourselves in relationship to one another is a goal of Creation. This is the reason Jesus said the key is that we must learn to love.

Becoming human and moving into this seemingly separate state of being was so shocking that we created a story to explain it. The story contained all the sadness we experienced because we felt so separate from our Creator. Over time, an extreme emotion known as guilt showed up in the story because of what had happened when the "separation" took place. Certainly it felt wrong to be separated in such a way from the Creator, but what if we didn't *do* anything wrong? What if this was the Divine Plan all along? What if it was necessary in order to create this world of duality, experience, choice and free will?

There's Only One Of Us Here

There was only one of us here in the beginning: God. There is still only one of us here when we view "us" from the perspective of Soul. We may look and act differently in these bodies, but we are not separate from God and we are not separate from one another in God.

Genesis Revisited

The Light is always shining inside of us. Even when it's covered up by darkness, sin, loveless perception and action, fear, doubt, and guilt — the Light inside still shines. God, the Creator, always remembers why this plan was set in motion. Even when we forget we are created in the Divine Image, even when we forget to love, God's Light is still there, waiting patiently for us to remember and return to the Divine embrace.

God is compassionate about our existence as human beings, but God does not seem to be overly concerned about or involved in the details, which are simply the learning process. And God is not offended by what we do, because God knows better. God needs no retaliation for any of our seemingly offensive actions, because we are not seen as perpetrators or victims in our experiences. Life is what it is: a learning experience for our eternal souls. God is not victimized by what we do, so God does not see us as victims. God is not wounded, so God does not see our wounds. God sees us in His perfect image and the experience of life goes on.

In human terms, one might say we are here to get our Ph.D. in life, and we are presenting our research and findings to The One who sent us to school and who awaits our return Home. I think of God as "The Godhead," the one who sits at Command Central gathering intelligence from our experiences. This view always brings me peace when I wonder why God doesn't save the innocent and the good and why evil seems to thrive on Earth.

God already knows that our story ends with victory — and Jesus tells us so — so it is easier to be patient while we discover the means by which we will return Home. The journey is more relaxing and much less stressful when you already know the happy ending. Jesus knew all of this, which is why he was capable of doing what he did for us.

Jesus, God in a body, willingly lived and then gave up his human life — the ultimate sacrifice — simply for love.

Made of God

When the people were about to stone him for blasphemy, Jesus said:

> Is it not written in your law, I said, Ye are gods? [87]

This proclamation was first revealed by God in the Old Testament, Psalms 82: "*I have said, Ye are gods; and all of you are children of the most High.*"[88] Jesus then reconfirmed this to the people. It's not easy for us to accept that a person can truly be made in the image of God. We killed Jesus for saying it. How much more difficult is it to accept this about ourselves? We have created elaborate excuses not to accept this truth. Now it is time.

> To give light to them that sit in darkness and in the shadow of death, to guide our feet into the way of peace.[89]

Yes, Jesus is saying that *we* are gods. Not God, but gods, as in "made of God," the image and embodiment of God. But as humans prone to self-denigration, we skip right over that part, because it is just too big, too much for us to accept. Instead

---

87	John 10:34
88	Psalm 82:6
89	Luke 1:79

we define ourselves as sinners and we diminish ourselves to avoid the responsibility God has given us. But the truth is, we begin and end in heaven, just like Jesus:

> And no man hath ascended up to heaven,
> but he that came down from heaven,
> even the Son of man which is in heaven.[90]

Jesus also said to the people and, therefore, to us now:

> You are the light of the world.[91]

We are often told that Jesus was the light of the world. Jesus said that *we* are the light of the world, too. And, in fact, Jesus said he was our example and we should do as he has done:

> For I have given you an example, that ye should
> do as I have done to you.[92]

Let's clear up some distinctions. It's important to remember that knowing we are made in the image of God does not mean there is no God, and it certainly never means that "I'm God and you're not." We must keep our ego and its attendant judgment and fear, in line with Spirit. God is the Creator, and we are the Beloved Creation, made in God's Image, and we were intended to create from the Divinity at our core.

---

90   John 3:13
91   Matthew 5:14
92   John 13:15

Second Coming

God, the Creator and God, the Created

We talked about God and creation during our Sunday night Bible Study. One of my friends, Katherine, said it this way: "There is God, the Creator, and there is God, the Created." Wow!

Why do we sometimes think that making ourselves small and unworthy somehow exalts God? Isn't it more empowering to see us collectively rising higher and higher, propelled by the Power of God inside us, as we learn and heal and grow? Then we can give even more Glory to God, the Creator, who shines ever more brightly. As we are called to act as God, the Created, we shine forth God's Divine Light.

God doesn't need us to be lower so that He can feel higher. God invites us daily to rise up. He already knows how high He is!

A Creation Story

Adam and Eve

The story of Adam and Eve has been told like this: The Almighty Creator of the entire universe spent the proverbial six days creating our beautiful planet and everything on it, saving his most precious creation (us) until the last day. He then took the seventh day off to rest and reflect on the magnificence of all that had been created. Then, when this new creation was just beginning, two tiny human beings disobeyed God, messed it all up, and were kicked out of paradise in about a minute. Really!?

I'm pretty sure God doesn't make mistakes and he was well aware of the Divine Plan he set in motion all those millennia ago. We just need to have a little faith about that — unless we prefer the arrogance of thinking that we, the tiny humans, are so powerful we could screw up God's finest Creation before it was even out of the beta test phase.

It makes more sense to me that the story of Adam and Eve is about the work God did to create our physical bodies, with the symbolism of eating the apple representing the solidification of the physical body into the physical world. This is a story about what it took to set this free-will system into motion. By giving us free will, God showed that even our Creator doesn't need to define us. Can't we give God that same consideration? Let's rejoice in the fact that we are God's Beloved Creation and then start acting like we know what that means!

This story has always been told as though Adam and Eve were powerful enough to screw everything up but were not powerful enough to help fix it. This parallels what we have already said about how we view ourselves when the ego is being sneaky in it's desire to control. Why do some people think the answer to every question about God is simply to illustrate how worthless *we* are? That perspective does not help us grow and thrive, and it is just wrong to interpret everything to prove that when God created us, he created junk. That is not humility. At the very least, that is ingratitude and, at worst, the height of arrogance. We are not capable of defining God or God's Creation.

Inherently Good

As a person of faith, I believe human beings are created in the image of God and are, therefore, inherently good. The American Heritage Dictionary defines the word "inherently" as *essentially characteristic or intrinsic — our essential nature.* As tempting as it is to focus on what human beings *do* that is good or evil, our inherent nature addresses the core of our being, not our actions. Humankind is intrinsically Divine, and each human being's core is made of God.

A Creation Story

The Book of Genesis says:

> Then God said, Let us make humankind in our image.[93]

We have no evidence that God has a physical body, except when incarnate, so this statement isn't about our bodies. It refers to the Divinity that *animates* the physical body — the Soul or Spirit — without which the physical body ceases to live.

The essential *nature* of humankind is Divine Spirit, and since a belief in God presupposes that God is good, it follows that human beings are inherently good, as well. However, we are also human, in that we each have a physical self, which houses the Soul. The body and the Soul work in symbiotic relationship in our lives.

It is difficult to examine our inherent nature without addressing the question, "If we are created in the image of God, why do people do bad things?" Interestingly, many of those who say we are inherently evil are also people of faith, but they do not seem to differentiate "how we are made" from "what we do." This duality creates an inner conflict that is at the heart of the human experience. Each of us always has a choice: striving to live in alignment with Divine Will — or following the ego, which is more aligned with survival, fear, and instant gratification.

Living in a free-will system necessitates making choices. If there were no choices to make, there would be no free will. What challenges us in the decision-making process is the fact that we are both human and Divine. When the physical self — body, mind, ego — is aligned with the Soul and

---

93   Genesis 1:26

inspired by a connection with the Divine, we are able to make choices that support our reason for being alive. When we align ourselves with the ego, then we are capable of the atrocities that lend strength to the argument that humankind must be inherently evil.

Because the Creator made us as beings of duality and set us free in a system that demands choice, we find ourselves experiencing lives that are fraught with pitfalls, but also ripe with opportunities for learning. It does not mean we are inherently evil when we make bad choices. Instead, isn't it possible that God created a system to teach us difficult lessons as a result of the choices we make?

To those who claim the story of Adam and Eve is proof that we are inherently evil, I suggest they re-examine their conclusion. I have to believe that the Almighty Creator was completely aware of what was happening in the Garden. God would not have spent all of his energy creating such a beautiful, intricate world only to allow us, mere mortals, to derail the whole thing with one bad choice. If this were the case, it would follow that humankind is both inherently evil *and* more powerful than God.

I propose a simpler explanation: that we were put here precisely so we would learn from our experiences, both good and bad. Perhaps we are doing *exactly* what God put us here to do, even though it sometimes seems like we're making a royal mess of things. We are inherently good *and* we often do bad things. This duality is at the core of the human experience. We are God's beloved creations, and he wants us to *learn to live from the Spirit that is inside each of us.*

A Creation Story

> ### *Inherently Evil?*
>
> One of my friends brought forward the question of our essential nature to her Bible Study group. She asked a large number of Christian women if they believed humans were inherently good or inherently evil. I was shocked when she told me the women agreed unanimously that humans are inherently evil. Perhaps this overwhelming belief is at the root of our problems. When we believe we are bad, we act out badly. What choice do we have, right? A shift in our perception is needed if there is any hope of us being saved from ourselves.

The New Covenant

Long before Jesus was born, we find in the Hebrew Bible (the Old Testament) that God said the day was coming when he would make a new covenant with the people and things would be different than they were before. (I have paraphrased the following verse to put it in a more modern context. Originally, the people listening to God were often referred to as *"the house of Israel and the house of Judah."* Readers today may or may not be of those houses, but we are all God's people.)

> Behold, the days come, saith the LORD, that I will make a new covenant: Not according to the covenant that I made with their fathers: But this shall be the covenant that I will make; After those days, saith the LORD, I will put my law in their inward parts, and write it in their hearts; and will be their God, and they shall be my people.[94]

---

94   Jeremiah 31:31-33

This gives us a promise — We all have the opportunity to know God from within us:

> And they shall teach no more every man his neighbour, and every man his brother, saying, Know the LORD: for they shall all know me, from the least of them unto the greatest of them, saith the LORD: for I will forgive their iniquity, and I will remember their sin no more.[95]

We are meant to shift to an inner focus, grounded in the Spirit of God that is our inherent nature. We no longer need to focus and rely only upon the teachings and outer doctrine of humankind, because we will begin to recognize the Word of God inside us.

This reliance on inner knowing is further confirmed:

> [God] also hath made us able ministers of the new testament; not of the letter, but of the spirit: for the letter kills, but the spirit gives life.[96]

In these and many other references in the Bible, God says the new covenant is in our *inward parts and written in our hearts*. This is The Christ — and this is what Jesus came to show us.

The Christ is awakening inside each one of us, and this is why it is time for us to stop squabbling over details that could be called "living only in the law." Doctrine is meant to be a tool to help us get to God. It is not meant to be more important than our individual relationships with God. Jesus taught that we need to live in the Spirit of Love. That means we must let go of our focus on sin

---

[95]   Jeremiah 31:34
[96]   2 Corinthians 3:6

and who is right and who is wrong and simply let ourselves *be in Christ*. It's not that we were doing it wrong before; maybe we just weren't ready. But God is saying we are ready now!

> Beloved, now are we the sons of God, and it doth not yet appear what we shall be: but we know that, when he shall appear, we shall be like him; for we shall see him as he is.[97]

In Christian tradition, this verse might be interpreted to mean that we shall be like him when the Messiah comes for the second time in human form. Or perhaps, it is when we die and go to Heaven. However, it is not a huge leap to realize that *"When he shall appear"* does not necessarily refer to a specific time or a specific person in a physical body who is coming to save us. As we speak of the Second Coming in the context of God saying *"I will put my law in their inward parts, and write it in their hearts"* and *"they shall know me,"* the Second Coming is also the shift from an outer to an inward focus. *"… When he shall appear …"* means that when Christ appears inside of us, we shall be like him. It is happening now.

We are then told that, because of this shift we will be changed into the image of the glory of the Lord:

> Now the Lord is that Spirit; and where the Spirit of the Lord is, there is liberty. But we all, with open face beholding as in a glass [mirror] the glory of the Lord, are changed into the same image from glory to glory, even as by the Spirit of the Lord.[98]

---

[97] 1 John 3:2
[98] 2 Corinthians 3:17-18

Here we are told that we will come to see the glory of God when we look into the mirror of God and see ourselves as the reflection of God. Said more simply, we will behold ourselves in the mirror and see God. Another beautiful parallel reminds us of how we mirror one another through our relationships: When we look into the "mirror" of another person and can see only the love of God reflecting back to us, we are experiencing The Christ in our daily human lives! This gives a whole new depth to the command, "Love your neighbor."

Namaste

It has become a fairly common practice in our culture to honor one another with Namaste. This is done by putting your hands together much like a child in prayer, with palms together and fingers pointing upward, with the base of the hands at the heart. We make a slight bow to another person and say "Namaste," which means "The God in me honors the God in you." I have also heard it said this way: "The Light in me honors the Light in you." Is this an example of The Christ awakening among us?

None of us know when this shift will happen in our own lives or in the world, but we are assured that it will happen.

> And he said unto them, It is not for you to know the times or the seasons, which the Father hath put in his own power. But ye shall receive power, after that the Holy Ghost is come upon you.[99]

---

99   Acts 1:7-8

A Creation Story

> The time is fulfilled, and the kingdom of
> God is at hand.[100]

* * * * *

> He that loves his life shall lose it; and he that
> hates his life in this world shall keep it
> unto eternal life.[101]

This verse tells us that even those who love their lives will lose their lives, because we all die eventually; this is simply a statement on the human condition. The second part of this verse, though, is necessary to examine. Some have interpreted it to mean that Jesus said we should hate our earthly lives. However, read it again and you can see that it says instead, "If you hate your life in this world you will keep *that hatred* into the next world." In terms of the New Covenant, if you hate your life you may have greater trouble making the shift and participating in God's Plan for our lives.

What we are doing here — in our bodies and in our lives — matters. We are not in charge of the timing, so our job is simply to show up and participate, always available for Spirit to move in and through us. It matters to God that we learn to be happy and at peace in this life as we prepare for what comes next, as we move from the old to the new:

> Therefore if any man be in Christ, he is a new
> creature: old things are passed away;
> behold, all things are become new.[102]

100	Mark 1:15
101	John 12:25
102	2 Corinthians 5:17

Developing a Spiritual Practice: What Do I Do?

I look for every opportunity I can find, and then I dig deeply into the experience for whatever golden nuggets I can discover. I remind myself that the Spirit of God is within and without. I face down my ego when it vies for control. I practice non-judgment (of myself and others) and remember to forgive. I pick up my power every chance I get. When I falter, I remind myself that I can't do it wrong, because even when I fall down, there is always a lesson to be learned that will help me be better the next time.

I do not focus on seeing myself as a sinner. This may be the most difficult challenge for some of you — to begin to see yourself only as a beautiful and cherished child of God. This should be easy, but it's not. Human nature tends to dwell on the negative, and we are conditioned by our culture to see ourselves as lacking, so feeling cherished and loved can take practice. For some of us, it takes a lot of practice! That's why I do what I do. It makes my life better and sweeter. It makes my life fuller, richer, and deeper. And this is why I am sharing my Gifts with you and why I encourage you to find your Gifts and share them with others. We find what we look for, so I look for God and Love all day long!

It's a process. It's a daily, living, healing practice that never ends unless you quit — and even then it doesn't really end, because God doesn't quit on us. But you will feel like you quit, and that will directly affect your life. My Dad taught me, "You can't fail if you won't quit." Those are wise words that I hold onto, especially when I feel like I can't go on any further.

My friend Ted thinks it is extraordinary that I work so diligently to strengthen my relationship with God. He says, "Most people aren't like you, Lily." It's true, I suppose, most people don't eat, breathe, and sleep God. To this I say, "Maybe I just need more help than most people." That's why I stay in constant contact with God. I don't do this because it's cool or because I'm special. I do this because I need it! My constant awareness of God in all things is what keeps my head above water.

The Next Beginning

What If Jesus Really is the Man at the Gas Station?

What if the Bible, when viewed from a slightly different perspective, shows us that Jesus talked about the Divine Awakening of humanity when he walked the Earth? What if this awakening is the Divine Plan that Jesus came here to seed and set in motion so that we could follow in his steps and become like him, awakened to love, and fulfilling our true Divine Purpose?

"God became man, so man might become Divine."[103] God knew it would take us time to overcome our attachment to our physical lives, bodies, and egos, so he left us all the tools and all the clues we would need to shift our awareness inwardly. God knows Divinity is within us, because he put it there, and he knew some of us would discover it and do our best to live from our inherently Divine core. He knew that, as we healed and began to see our physical lives from a Divine Perspective, some of us would take the risk and tell others. He knew the momentum would build and we would be moved one step closer to realizing that this was God's Plan for us all along.

---

103   Athanasius

Second Coming

Baby step after baby step, we are awakening to our birthright as beings created in the Divine Image. We are becoming free of the doubts and fears that come with these fragile bodies and frightened egos, and we are awakening to the importance of being in love with ourselves, in love with one another, and in love with God.

One by one, we are awakening to The Christ, and we are learning to live in the idea of eternal life while still existing in these bodies. We are learning to love our enemies, our neighbors, and ourselves from a place of Grace. This is not just an idea given to us by a distant God; it has emerged from within, where God planted the seeds of love on the day we were created.

What if God really does use all things for good, and there are no mistakes?

What if we cannot do it wrong?

What if God doesn't count sins, preferring only to recognize acts of loving kindness?

What if all we have to do is wake up each day in gratitude for our very lives and then go out and act from that gratitude in every way possible throughout our days?

What if we are here to create Heaven on Earth, right here and right now?

What if we don't go anywhere — and afterlife is simply the synergistic creation of all we do here?

What if we are here to experience and choose and participate in Divine Creation, doing our part to create the New Being, the new Heaven, and the new Earth that is spoken about in the Book of Revelation?

The Bridge

Many people did not believe Jesus was the Messiah who came to Earth to speak as God. Some were content to view him simply as a great teacher, but others were threatened by how many people had begun to follow in his footsteps. In the Book of Acts, the great rabbi Gamaliel speaks to the other leaders of the temple, giving them guidance on what to do about the spread of the teachings of this man Jesus, whom they do not believe to be the Messiah. The leaders thought the teachings of Jesus would be silenced when they killed him, but his followers continued to spread the message. Some of the priests wanted to kill all of them, too. Gamaliel said the followers of Jesus, who claimed to speak from God, should not be harmed:

> And now I say unto you, Refrain from these men, and let them alone: for if this counsel or this work be of men, it will come to naught: But if it be of God, ye cannot overthrow it; lest haply ye be found even to fight against God.[104]

In this verse, Gamaliel is saying, "If what is being said is simply the work of humans, it will come to nothing, so don't worry about it. On the other hand, if the words are truly from God, there is nothing that can be done to stop it." He further points out that, if this work *is* coming from God, they wouldn't want to stop it anyway. Treat what I have shared with you likewise. If what I have said here is merely the rambling of an errant human mind, it will come to nothing. And if these words

---

104   Acts 5:38-39

and ideas came through Christ and are from our Creator, then we are all truly blessed by God's Grace to have received them.

I see myself standing in the middle of a bridge with the Christians on one side and the Spiritual People on the other. At first I have my hands extended out to either side, since I embrace both of these traditions in my personal relationship with God. And then God says, "Lily, bring your hands together at your heart, in Namaste, as in prayer." The message is clear: We are meant to come together in the loving embrace of God, no matter where we are standing on the bridge.

The Last Shall Be First

I'm not the first to share the ideas contained within this book. I'm one of many people throughout the ages who have said and are still saying, "Yes, God, I Am here and I love what you have created and I will keep believing. I will be in service to God in all forms and I will continue to pray, as I have prayed for so long, 'Help me prove that love wins,' until the Second Coming saves the whole world."

You may be wondering: if so many people already think this way, when will the Second Coming happen and what is taking so long? I was introduced to an idea long ago in my spiritual journey that addresses the notion of reaching critical mass as it relates to the Awakening of The Christ. By definition, critical mass refers to the smallest amount necessary to set off a chain reaction. As each new person awakens, another grain of sand is added to the Love side, the Christ side, of the scale, until finally the scale tips and everything shifts.

How many grains of sand does it take before the scales tip and humankind is transformed into a newly awakened life form — with Divine Will at its center and God's Divine love as its core? How many of us need to wake up and know that we are truly created in the Image of God, right here and right now, and that all we have to do is know it and live from it?

There is no way to know the exact number until we reach it, but I find it interesting that it will be the *last* one of us to awaken who creates critical mass, causing everything to shift. The last one is the Messiah of the Second Coming. Yes, the *last* grain of sand will cause the scales to tip, but *it cannot happen without all the others who go first*. Each of us is called to participate in this synergistic process of co-creating Heaven on Earth. Each person is called to be in service to The One, The Christ Consciousness, which is made fully manifest when enough of us awaken to make it possible. Only then — and ultimately only together — will humanity truly be saved.

No one will actually know when we reach critical mass. No one will know who is the last one to awaken, because the shift will already have occurred in that one holy instant. It is remarkable and critically important that we will not know the identity of that last one, because the last time someone said he was The Christ, we killed him. This time, with the Second Coming, everything will be different.

For now, we are all simply in service to The Christ, The Divine. We are the ones who awakened "before the beginning" and the last one to awaken will truly save us all. In this way, *"the last shall be first"*[105] in the newly awakened world, *"the New Heaven and the New Earth."*[106]

It can't be me who is last, because clearly we are not there yet. And if we had already awakened en masse, I wouldn't be writing this book at all. So, who is it? Who is the *last* to awaken so The Christ reigns in love and grace eternally?

Ah, I see ... is it you?

Thank you very much.

---

105   Matthew 19:30
106   Revelation 21:1 *And I saw a new heaven and a new earth: for the first heaven and the first earth were passed away; and there was no more sea.*

www.ingramcontent.com/pod-product-compliance
Lightning Source LLC
Chambersburg PA
CBHW020109020526
44112CB00033B/1102